THE LOVING
PUSH

How parents and professionals can help
spectrum kids become successful adults

Temple Grandin, Ph.D.

Professor of Animal Sciences, Colorado State University

Debra Moore, Ph.D.

Psychologist, Sacramento, CA

The Loving Push: How parents and professionals can help spectrum kids become successful adults

All marketing and publishing rights guaranteed to and reserved by:

FUTURE HORIZONS INC.

721 W Abram St, Arlington, TX 76013
800-489-0727 (toll free)
817-277-0727 (local)
817-277-2270 (fax)
E-mail: *info@fhautism.com*
www.fhautism.com

© 2015 Temple Grandin and Debra Moore
Cover design by Robert Morrow
Cover illustration courtesy of iStock/Getty Images
Interior design by John Yacio III
All rights reserved.
Printed in Canada.

Photo of Temple Grandin © Rosalie Winard.

ISBN: 9781941765203

*To our mothers, Eustacia Cutler and
Alma Rebecca Moore, who invariably
provided loving pushes, some appreciated
at the time, others not so much.*

In retrospect, we are extremely grateful.

In memory of Oliver Sacks, M.D. (1933 – 2015)

CONTENTS

FOREWORD

By Temple Grandin, Ph.D.

Mother knew that she had to "stretch" and lovingly push me just outside my comfort zone so I could develop to my fullest. She was always urging me to try new things but she made sure there were no surprises, because a sudden introduction of something new was scary. I was lucky to get into a good speech therapy program at age 2½ and after I learned to talk, she always gave me many opportunities to use my speaking skills. In our family, all the children had to do the job of party hostess and host. At age seven or eight, I had to put on my best clothes and greet the guests who had been invited over for dinner. This taught important skills such as shaking hands and greeting people. My two younger sisters and brother also had to greet all the guests and help serve the snacks. In the 1950's, all children were taught social skills in a much more structured manner. My brother hated being a party host, but later in life, he admitted that it helped him talk to older men. This helped him become a senior vice president of a large bank. Even the normal kids benefitted from practicing learning to greet and talk to new people.

Debra Moore and I decided to collaborate on this book because we are both seeing more instances where fully verbal older children and young adults with ASD (autistic spectrum disorder) are not learning crucial basic skills for socializing and employment. We are both very worried about these youth, because without these skills, they are unlikely to be able to lead successful, independent, satisfying adult lives. If parents, teachers, and therapists of all sorts recognize the danger zones for these children, however, we can turn this around. That is our intent in writing this book.

At many different conferences, I am seeing a pattern of four things that are preventing smart children and adults with ASD from making a successful transition to full independence. Debra has seen these same concerns in the youth and families she worked with. These four things are a result of changes happening in our families, schools, and the world of technology.

1. ASD youth are being overprotected and not given enough opportunities to learn how to do things on their own. Too frequently, parents, teachers, or aides do things for the child that deprive him or her of the opportunity to make mistakes and thereby learn to solve problems on their own. For example, when I give talks, I meet teenagers with good speaking skills, but their parent does all the talking for the child. One time a mom started to ask a question for her child, and I said, "Your child needs to ask the question." In this and most cases, I have been able to coax the child to talk, even in front of many people. They are then happy that they were able to do it. To help the child keep his nerve, I will warn the audience to hold applause until after the child has responded. Many kids with ASD just need additional time to get their words out.

   I think moms often run interference for their children because they are afraid their child will be hurt when he/she makes a mistake. But to learn and grow, you have to make some mistakes. For example, my first attempt at teaching a class when I was in graduate school was a disaster. I panicked and walked out. To solve this problem, the next time I had prepared really good slides so if I panicked, I could fall back on them.

2. Our educational system has changed. Too many schools have removed the hands-on classes where many ASD or ADHD children or teenagers can excel. Classes such as art, music, cooking, sewing, woodworking, theatre, electrical repair, welding, and auto repair expose students to careers. A student cannot determine whether or not he likes something if they are never exposed to it. Patrick Stewart, who played Captain Picard on *Star Trek*, developed his love of acting when he was 12 and had the experience of performing in a school play.

   Our kids need exposure both to open their eyes to options, and also to give them some preliminary experience in different things that could lead to a career. Parents and other adults in their lives have to take over what the schools used to do. We have to get our kids introduced to adults working in fields that could lead to careers. Some really good jobs where kids could excel are computer programming, skilled trades such as auto mechanics, and careers in the arts. Computer coding and the skilled trades are two areas where employers are having a hard time finding sufficiently qualified workers. These are areas of job opportunities.

We can take our children's special interests and broaden them to many areas with potential for work. For example, if a teenager likes cars, we can use that interest to improve their reading (giving them auto magazines or instruction manuals), their math, and even physics.

3. Too many students with ASD are graduating from high school without having learned basic life skills they need as a young adult. These skills are necessary if they plan to attend college, get a job, or live independently without supervision. Some of these fundamental skills are driving or navigating public transportation, reliably being on time, having good social manners, maintaining basic hygiene, being able to follow instructions, seeing tasks through to completion, and being able to receive feedback appropriately.

We can prepare our children by having them do household chores from an early age, and do paid or volunteer work outside the home once they reach their teenage years. We have devoted a chapter to how to help your child learn these basics so they can succeed at work, in college, and maintaining a household.

4. Excessive video game playing has derailed too many kids. Too often I hear a parent tell me "He's 21 and he won't leave the bedroom." We are now discovering that those on the autism spectrum are especially vulnerable to obsessive gaming to the point of addiction. Our book has an extensive chapter on how to prevent problem video gaming and how to work with it if a child, teen, or adult has already become addicted.

The "Loving Push": Some More Examples

The purpose of this book is to help parents let go and give careful, loving pushes to get their child to try new things. Before we delve into the main part of the book, I would like to tell some additional anecdotes of getting a fully verbal child to do something new.

One time I was at a dinner with about eight people, and one family had brought their young teenage son who had been diagnosed with ASD. He had good speech, but like many kids who have had many things done for them, he clung to his mom and did not greet me. Since he only liked to eat certain things, his mom had brought take-out food to the dinner so he would not have to eat the food that was being served. After the dinner started, he proceeded to eat the take-out meal with his hands. At this point I said, "This is a formal dinner, use the utensils." The child immediately picked up the fork and started to use it. He ate the entire meal with utensils and even tried some of the other food.

This is a good example of a "teachable moment." When the child started to eat with his hands, I gave the instruction on what he should do. The mistake that is often made is for parents and teachers to say "no" instead of giving the instruction, which tells the child what he should do. A common pattern I have observed is that moms sometimes overprotect and dads want to see if the child is capable of more. After the boy successfully used the utensils, his dad gave me a "high five."

The Importance of Opportunities to Learn Work Skills

During one of my many endless delays at airports, I had the opportunity to talk to a family who had a teenage boy who was really good at doing computer animation. The boy was shy but he was willing to talk to me about his work, and he showed me some of it that was on his tablet. When I have done talks at technology companies, I have seen many adults similar to him; kind of shy, but making a good living. With both parents, I discussed how their son's abilities in animation could be used to create a summer experience that would teach important work skills. A big problem I am seeing with teen boys on the spectrum is that they are spending too much time alone in their room playing video games or some other pursuit. This kid needed some activities to get him out of the house. All that is needed is a little ingenuity to find something for him to do right in the neighborhood.

One member of the family commented that the pastor at their church had some video of a church picnic that needed editing and titles. This would be a great opportunity for their son, to get him accustomed to doing work outside the home. I suggested that the work should be done at the church offices. It is essential that he learn how to do work that somebody else wants. Mom admitted that she had a hard time letting go, even though the church was close by and he had already ridden there on his bike. I told her she needs to let go because the "birdies" have to learn to fly and develop.

When I was a teenager, I was never allowed to become a recluse in my room. I had to be at meals, attend church, and participate in family gatherings. Sometimes children with ASD have sensory problems that may need some accommodation, but too often the problem is parents who are afraid to give their child a chance to stretch their wings. A quiet office in a church is not going to have anything that would overwhelm her son's senses, or be dangerous. The opportunity to edit somebody else's video was an excellent example of a safe work experience outside the home. He will be able to start learning to use his creativity to make some original video for the show titles and edit the already existing footage into a show many will enjoy. This will require accepting instructions and thinking about what the entire congregation would want to see.

Mother had a natural instinct and knew how to stretch me in increments without causing too much stress. When I was a teenager, my mother thought going to my aunt's ranch in Arizona would be a good experience to try something new. At first I was afraid to go. She gave me a choice. Choices are very important for children with ASD. It's also essential to remember that sudden surprises can cause great fear. I knew about the trip to my aunt's ranch months before I went there. I had telephone conversations with my aunt and I was given pictures of the ranch long before I went there. It was not a surprise. Surprises scare.

My choice was I could either go to the ranch for a week or stay all summer. Once I got there, I loved it and stayed all summer. There was always an opportunity for choice, but staying alone in my room in my house was never allowed. Providing choices, combined with advance preparation, gives a child a sense of control so that he can handle new life-expanding experiences.

INTRODUCTION

By Debra Moore, Ph.D.

Our children on the spectrum are growing up. According to Drexel University's National Autism Report, about 50,000 kids with autism exit high school each year in the U.S. About a half million youth with autism will enter adulthood over the next decade. This book springs from our passion, aspirations, and hopes for these teens and young adults.

We want to increase the odds that your child grows into an adult with a rewarding, meaningful life. We want them to live at their highest and best capacity. We support them in defining and achieving an individualized and productive definition of success and satisfaction. We hope they have the opportunity to express their unique perspectives, personalities, and strengths. To achieve these goals, they need mentors, guidance, and support. They also need structure, appropriate expectations, and frequent "loving pushes."

We believe that parents, professionals, and community members can greatly influence the odds of this next generation's success. We can all help guide and inspire our children to become adults with meaningful, productive lives. And if we succeed, everyone stands to greatly benefit.

Throughout history, many of our planet's most revolutionary advances have resulted from the unique perspectives, brilliance, and creativity of those on the autism spectrum. Einstein's theory of relativity and Henry Cavendish's groundbreaking theories on the properties of electricity and heat are two striking examples. Less conspicuous, but equally meaningful, workplaces, community organizations, and families have been enhanced by the exemplary dedication, focus, and loyalty of autistic adults.

From each of our unique perspectives, we've witnessed children and teens on the spectrum take a variety of paths as they reach adulthood. We have seen some lives wasted or lived below their true potential. Some teens remain unemployed and living at home, even though they are intelligent and capable of making a contribution. They have not learned the vital skills needed to navigate the adult world. Too many are languishing in bedrooms, in front of their computer, compulsively playing and replaying online video games.

It doesn't have to turn out this way. Both of us have witnessed many youth on the spectrum find productive and meaningful adult lives. Their journeys came in endless varieties, but had several factors in common. The outcomes didn't happen by luck, and the successes didn't happen without the help of others. Wise adults, who provided guidance, nurturance, and direction, influenced them. Most importantly, they were exposed to opportunity. Their accomplishments were the result of persistence and hard work by both the child and others. And they followed a vital rule. Each child and teen built a foundation of practical, real-world skills, and then they found a niche that fit their own personal strengths, passions, and ways of thinking.

As a parent, your aim is to build both your child's character and competency. You have been attempting that since they were little. If your "child" is now a teen or even an adult, they need you in new ways. Many times in the past, they've needed you to protect them. Now it's time for a loving developmental push. It's time for new skills on both their end and yours.

Transitioning from adolescence into adulthood brings both unfamiliar challenges and unique opportunities. We want to give parents of younger children pre-emptive help so they can start now to best prepare for the years ahead. For parents of older children, we want to give you information you can use right now to increase the odds of a successful transition to adult life. With more and more young adults on the spectrum entering adulthood every day, we don't have time to lose.

First, we'll introduce you to the real stories of some men and women on the spectrum. Ranging in age from 18 to 57, they haven't always had an easy time of it. Parents or other special people in their lives provided support, opportunity, and guidance. They are now creating meaningful adult lives that embrace and accentuate their unique strengths and passions. Details of the journeys they and their families took will be used throughout the book to help you better envision keys to your child's success.

We'll then tell you how to help your child have a positive mindset. We'll also help you recognize potential minefields and how to work around them. We'll give you concrete examples showing how to teach your teen specific skills they'll need in the real, adult world.

The individuals profiled here may or may not resemble your child. Autism is by definition a disorder that occurs along a spectrum, and therefore affects everyone differently. It can result in a wide range of challenges and strengths. Other diagnoses, such as ADD/ADHD, often accompany ASD or are mistaken for ASD due to similar behaviors. Don't get too caught up in labels. If you recognize aspects of your child in this book, take the ideas and recommendations and run with them.

No matter what age your child is, or what label they have, it's important to remember that what abilities you see today may not be what you see tomorrow. Adult "success" comes in many flavors, just as each child does. The common denominator is a life lived to one's own unique, full capacity. Success is not measured or determined by IQ, verbal fluency, or physical ability.

Success is steered by hope, determination, and discovery. Not every child will end up where the individuals profiled here did, and that's not the point. But all children should have hopes and dreams, and the opportunity to choose and lead meaningful and satisfying lives. With the support, intervention, and "loving pushes" of family and others, these dreams can come true.

A NOTE ABOUT TERMINOLOGY

We want to make a couple of points about terms we have used in this book.

One is that while we use terms like *ASD* (autism spectrum disorder) and *NT* (neurotypical), we emphatically believe that no person can be simplified and captured in a label. Even when labels are useful for purposes of description and for accessing resources, they only reflect part of a person, not their essence.

Second, we have frequently used the terms "kid" or "child" in this book. This made sense to us for two reasons: we thought it would be less cumbersome to you than repeatedly reading "child, teen, or adult," plus we thought parents would understand that no matter what chronological age, one's offspring will always be your "child."

We believe that the lessons and suggestions in this book apply to all ages. We encourage you to use them with "kids" of any chronological age. Our goal is that parents, teachers, professionals, and anyone else who cares about an individual on the spectrum begins to lovingly guide, push, and mentor them as early as possible, and for as long as feasible.

PART I

The Path to Success
Starts Here:
Restoring Hope

CHAPTER 1

Real Stories, Real Successes: 8 Inspiring Profiles

SCOTT, 28

Former Quality Assurance Tester at Aspyr Media
Diagnosed with Asperger's

Scott is a good example of how teens can turn themselves around and move from stagnation to action. His vocational journey also illustrates the need for preparing realistically for the workforce and the need to acquire skills that are transferable.

> I was diagnosed with Asperger's when I was 12. I was pretty typical and I had restricted interests and social struggles. School was tough. High school was hell! I thought of it as a grinding mosh pit where everyone is terrible to everyone else. I spent pretty much all of my time just hanging out with a band of guys who constantly played video games. I really loved video games. I turned to them to escape, and then they took hold and I sank into a hole of video quicksand.

Scott could easily have become mired in a world of compulsive gaming. The next part of his story illustrates how much influence others can have in helping a floundering teen find a positive direction.

So I was this listless 15-year-old, and I was thinking I was pretty terrible at everything. I had no idea what I was going to do. Then one evening my Dad took me to a dinner party. Believe me, I would have rather stayed home playing video games! So at dinner this guy turns to me and says, "Figure out what you really love to do. Then find someone who will pay you to do it." Well, you already know playing video games is what I loved to do. But for the first time it occurred to me that video games are a "product." And that somebody has to make them. And I asked myself, "Who are the people who make these games?"

Once Scott saw the potential of putting his special interest to good use, he needed guidance to make it a reality.

I talked to my parents. My mom scoured classified ads and finally spotted one for a video game tester. I didn't even have a resume at that point, but I wrote up everything I could about what I knew about video games and I got an interview! And that resulted in getting a gig each year from the time school let out until it started up again in the fall. For three years I worked summers at a game publisher doing quality assurance.

After high school, Scott started college. Because English had been his easiest high school subject, that's what he automatically majored in. But he had no idea what to do with it. And more importantly, he almost lost sight of pursuing his special interest. Fortunately, he again listened to someone else's input.

I had a college roommate who was a fellow gamer. He was from Austin, Texas, and told me "Hey, there are lots of gamers back there!" He told me Silicon Valley, where we were, was big on software but wasn't the center of the gaming universe. He said Austin was where I should relocate and find a job. He was moving back there himself, so I agreed. Having him there turned out to be critical for both my personal and professional success. I needed a landing pad and a safe, comfortable place to come home to. And the gaming community in Austin is insular. Everybody knows everybody. That was really helpful. But if I hadn't paid my dues with the summer jobs, I probably wouldn't have been competitive.

Until just before this book went to press, Scott worked full time as a video game "debugger." He said his job was the perfect union of his ASD traits and his special passion. The following quote was from before he was laid off from that job.

> I get to work on broken video games all day long. I'm part of a cycle of people who each have their own important part in making the games a successful product people can enjoy. You've got talented creative people who envision the game, then the coder people who make the characters work, and then people like me who identify the parts that are broken. We enter "bug reports" into databases.
>
> We play one game eight hours a day repeatedly and keep an eye out for anything that is broken. So maybe we spot that the hero's sword has turned into a pineapple! We send it back to the developer because obviously they got the code string mixed up and missed it. And they send it back to us, but now the hair is purple instead of brown! So we spot that and send it back again. It's an endless cyclic iteration—extremely repetitive, detail-oriented, and immensely routine. All traits that work great for me!

Even though Scott loved his job, he and his family have learned things they think are very important to convey to others on the spectrum. His mom emailed after Scott was laid off, with advice for other parents.

> We've realized that quality assurance (QA) testing of video games will almost always be a minimum-wage contract-only position, since there are so many people who want to do that job. There is no career ladder here. Many testers would like to get into creating games, but with the advent of so many academic training programs for that field now, testers may be at a disadvantage compared to applicants who have those specific degrees. It's also a field prone to booms and busts and frequent layoffs, even for game developers. For people on the spectrum, that

amount of change can be stressful. That said, it's still a good job for a young adult to gain basic job skills like responsibility, attention to detail, organization, and interaction. We're encouraging Scott to articulate the skills he learned and apply for positions in QA in different industries, where there may be more stability. I want parents who read this book and might think video game testing or QA is the perfect job for their spectrum kid to also realize the drawbacks.

Scott agreed with his mom and elaborated in a phone call. He's now in the process of expanding his career search and has his own advice for his peers.

What Mom said is true—it's an industry driven by booms and busts, and the vast majority of entry-level positions are six-month contracts. One would have to be very lucky to find one that's not. I got very lucky and knew it, because before this job I had two that were just short-term contracts. So I naively (in retrospect) thought I'd have more job security in this non-contract position. But after awhile, I noticed there weren't many opportunities to move up. Then recently, the company said they were shifting to a "more transparent" system of evaluations and promotions. They said if you showed competencies you'd be a strong candidate to move up to the next tier, but the flip side was that if you weren't ready, you were let go. My friend was laid off the same day I was.

Scott's also not sure what to make of some feedback he received in his evaluation. He thought he was doing quite well and that something that had been brought to his attention earlier was no longer an issue.

They said I came across as defensive at work. That was strange to me. I thought that whenever somebody came to me with a question about my work, I'd explain why I did whatever it was. I usually thought I had done what they wanted me to do, so I'd remind them what they'd said to me. That behavior was coming across as overly defensive and they thought I couldn't take criticism. I got that feedback twice, but I thought I'd done enough to rectify it. At the end of one meeting they even said it was okay and that it could be worked out. I thought it had been fixed. I told them to let me know if anything else is a problem and nothing was said, but in the final meeting they told me I wasn't ready to move up so they were letting me go, and they also said that five months ago we talked to you about your defensiveness and you didn't improve. It felt unfair to me and I feel a little bitter.

Scott believes working in video game QA was very good in some ways, and says he learned some essential job skills. But he warns others who are interested in the general field of gaming that there are significant limitations, and he shared some excellent advice he said was passed on to him from a friend.

I don't know if very many people want to be testing games at age 40, but the fact is it's a dead end for those with ambitions beyond QA. So now I'm between jobs and looking at more generalized software companies. I found out about a small producer of a global application that sounds interesting and I am in communication with them. My advice to others is to network. The usual advice of "bring passion and your best effort" isn't enough. That's necessary for any job. You have to have realistic expectations. And you'll need to bring independent creativity to the table in this field. Creating games is a very common dream but the reality is somewhat different. My friend had this good advice: "If you want a road to lead you somewhere different you have to change too. If you don't change where you are going, you will continue going where you are headed." I think that's good life path advice.

MARINA, 33
Married and mother of a daughter
Diagnosed with Asperger's

Marina's mother recalls their pediatrician being confused by her daughter. He told her that her child might be in and out of prison or spend her life locked in a mental institution. He bluntly proclaimed that Marina would never be able to take care of herself.

> So I feared for her safety and her future. I was afraid she could never be sympathetic to others and that she'd stay dissociated from people, society, and the basic rules we have to follow in order to succeed in life. Everything was black and white for Marina. There were no grays, no in-betweens, and no middle ground. If something didn't catch her interest, she would not participate in or care about it. She had no friends and couldn't read people's social signals, gestures, or even their words. She didn't hear complete conversations.

Marina recollects being depressed and anxious for as long as she can remember. As a child she struggled with loud noises and didn't want to be touched. She would pull away or make a "mean face" if someone unexpectedly touched her. She found most people shallow and felt like they knew hidden "crazy algorithms or secret formulas" that she had no clue about.

School was hard for Marina. She was afraid of both kids and teachers. Her mother set out to build her confidence and academic skills at the same time.

> We would do spelling drills and I expected her to get A's because I knew she could. But at first she would spell the word as though she was asking a question. I told her if she said it in a "question voice," I'd mark it wrong. I wanted her to learn to spell but also to learn to speak with confidence!
>
> I thought it was important for her to analyze, not just obey. I wanted her to develop more than one way of perceiving the world. So I would have close her eyes and pretend she was blind. Then I would hand her something —like an apple—and have her describe it many different ways, asking, "How do you know it is an apple?" She learned to use all her senses and to figure things out on her own.
>
> I also wanted her to learn to analyze people. I told her that her teachers were smart, but they were just people, and all people make mistakes.

I told her to obey them (and me, and Sunday school teachers) when they asked her to do good things. But I also told her to think for herself. She started analyzing her teachers without realizing it.

Later, when she was older, she and her sisters used to take really long walks through different neighborhoods. This was after her father and I divorced, and for a time we were actually homeless. We lived in an old van, usually by a public park. The girls would walk to upscale neighborhoods and look in the windows, and they started interacting with the people who lived there. Marina would come back and describe what she had seen. Her curiosity and approach of "analyzing" her world was paying off socially.

Her teachers, however, thought Marina was a "problem" and considered her "rebellious" because she wouldn't always verbally respond to them. In sixth grade, the principal told Marina's mother her daughter would no longer be allowed to attend his school because they were unable to help her. Her mother decided to find a different route.

I knew Marina was smart, but her anxiety and daydreaming kept her from learning. I finally started home schooling her. We spent time on the computer, and that suddenly opened a whole new world to her—she could view, learn about, and even buy things! She started reading others' opinions, got exposure to other lifestyles and interests, and enjoyed educating and entertaining herself through the Internet.

Yet, today, Marina's mother looks back and wishes she had done even more.

I wish I had pushed harder. I wish I had forced the school system to help. I wish I had acquired more knowledge to help Marina. I wish I had pushed her a little harder and put her into situations that would have taught social skills—maybe speaking, drama, or etiquette classes. I think I sometimes made excuses for her. I could have pushed her more to explain her thoughts or feelings. All children should be encouraged and nudged to do well. Until something is tried, you'll never know what a child or adult is capable of. Children will become adults. They must function safely within society.

Marina has built a satisfying life that includes a husband and daughter. She makes contributions to her community and to the family's finances, and is continuing her education.

I run a volunteer feeding program for the homeless every Saturday. We do it as a family. I also just recently started volunteering at the SPCA. I really enjoy helping people. It makes me feel really good that I am a positive force in someone else's life—that I'm helping make someone's life a little better. Having a strong adherence to routines helps me get up and out when I otherwise don't feel like it. When I'm sick or fatigued I am able to push past that because it's Saturday and we have to feed the homeless today.

I have always had an interest in astronomy since my childhood. My older sister bought us a computer when I was 14 and she got us connected to the Internet via dial up and AOL. At first we didn't really understand the Internet—we would just click on whatever links popped up on the home page. Then we discovered the search engine feature.

I started researching anything I had questions about—a very wide variety of topics from the behavior of wolves to boa constrictors, Nile monitors, and komodo dragons, as well as fish and game regulations, gun laws, infectious diseases, neurology, and forensic anthropology.

Then I happened to watch a movie about physics and became interested in that. After further Internet research, I discovered and became fascinated with astrophysics. Right now I'm in my second year at a community college, majoring in physics, and doing well. I still find it hard to concentrate in a classroom though, so I rely primarily on textbooks and the Internet to understand material. I'm really fascinated by the universe and want to transfer to UC Berkeley when I finish here. I plan to major in Astrophysics with a minor in Computer Science.

I take care of the entire bill-paying for the family and it's my job to plan our budget. I enjoy budgeting and managing our finances. Learning as a kid to create shopping lists and use a calculator paid off. Right now my financial contribution to the family comes from breeding and selling rats—another subject I also learned from various Internet sites.

JAIME, 35
From Coder to Project Manager, to Business Analyst at a large technology company
Diagnosed with PDD-NOS/High Functioning Autism

Jaime has found success with one of the world's largest technology companies. His work involves almost daily interactions with others, which he still finds challenging. He enjoys the routine of his job and he likes the pay. As he's been there longer, however, he's started to wish his tasks were even more technical, and feels that he is not utilizing all of his skills.

Being on the autism spectrum actually helps me in my job. I am meticulous about anything technical. I am also able to view problems and solutions with a completely different perspective than others.

Earlier in his life, Jaime's school performance looked fine to outsiders, but he knew that he was not putting forth effort that matched his abilities. He managed to get by, and even received some awards because he is very bright. But he wasn't motivated and often didn't even bother to read assignments fully.

I was smart and could get B's in classes without even reading the full chapters of school textbooks. I thought I was "too smart to study." At the time that was satisfactory to me. I underachieved.

Moreover, he said he was always the social outsider and was subjected to bullying.

I was always the outcast and I was never confident within groups. I got teased a lot. The kids taunted me with names like "cabezon" (big head) and "orejon" (big ears). I eventually learned that the opinions and actions of bullies don't matter. After gaining that confidence, it was much easier to avoid them.

It probably didn't help that Jaime struggled with neurological glitches that sometimes made it difficult to process incoming information and to regulate motor skills.

As a child I struggled to process what others were trying to tell me. I was also challenged with motor apraxia—a neurological condition that makes it hard to plan or produce body movements upon request or command. These are still areas that require great effort to deal with. I make sure to really absorb what someone is telling me before I respond.

Now, as an adult, Jaime has been in a live-in, committed relationship for the past four years. He credits his girlfriend as his greatest positive influence. Socially, he says he was always an introvert and still prefers just a small number of friends.

My partner has helped me so much in understanding NT (neurotypical) mentality. She explains the "whys" with logic and rationale in addition to appealing to my sensibilities. With a lot of training, she has helped me perform mundane tasks in a logical fashion, meanwhile acknowledging my unique talents.

Because I find it difficult to understand social contexts and cues, my attempts at increasing my social world have not really worked out well. I prefer to have just a few friends. These friends do not seem to care about adhering to social norms and they accept me for my uniqueness.

Jaime has also struggled with problems in his relationship that resulted from his intense interest in online video gaming.

I enjoy playing online games and it sometimes becomes a problem. My partner noticed that I get too zoned into the game, and she has brought it to my attention. Once I am in the game, I cannot easily leave its grasp on my attention. She has helped teach me how to pay attention to what other things are going on around me in addition to the game.

Jaime lives independently and finds some aspects of adult life easier than others.

I have never had any difficulty living on my own. I manage my money and do quite well at it. I shop for myself but do have difficulty discerning what is fashionable and what is not. I taught myself enough cooking to get by, but rarely do it. My housekeeping isn't exactly spotless, but my places of residence were never really messy. I don't notice minor splotches or messes when vacuuming or cleaning the bathroom, but I've improved over time in that area.

MARTHA, 57
Clerk in the Science Department at Sacramento City College
Diagnosed with Asperger's

In my mid 30s a therapist I was seeing told me I might have Asperger's and I asked him what I could do about it. He said, "Nothing." At that time there was no Internet and it did not occur to me to research it further. Since "nothing could be done about it," I thought the diagnosis was useless at the time and just put it out of my mind. Then a few years later I heard about Asperger's again during an NPR story about Temple Grandin. By then, I was able to go online to learn more. I realized I had finally found the explanation for the difficulties I have had all my life.

A different therapist, who treats others on the spectrum, then confirmed my diagnosis a few years later. I also deal with depression and anxiety and most likely some ADHD.

Martha learned important life skills as a teen and young adult.

> My first volunteer work was visiting patients at a nursing home when I was about 16. Later, in my 20s, I helped tutor people who were learning English. I've kept up volunteer work throughout my life. For many years I worked with Friends of the California State Fair. I prepared the monthly newsletter and was the board secretary at one point. I have also been active in church and still help out as an usher.

Martha's family background was not very nurturing, but she recalls two positive influences outside her family. When one became increasingly sexually inappropriate with her, she ended the relationship, but she still credits him with teaching her important life and work skills.

> There was a man I worked for when I was a teenager in the 1970s. At the time I needed a job and was going into as many shops as I could looking for one. I would go repeatedly if they said "no" the first time. The third time I went into this man's shop he hired me, saying he was impressed that I was so persistent. It was a radio and TV repair shop, back in the days when there were lots of shelves full of "tubes" that had to be stored and inventoried. I understood the work quickly and was a natural because it required a lot of attention to detail. I wasn't as good with customer service, but he taught me how to appropriately answer the phone and interact with customers.

Martha has struggled socially, but at this point in her life has found a comfortable amount of connection with others through her work and with members of her church.

> I developed absolutely no friendships during my college days. I have never been in a romantic or sexual relationship. I have had female friends off and on over the years.
>
> Often when I am in a group, I feel that I am invisible. Or that I talk too much and people just tolerate or ignore me. I do not enjoy parties

or other group activities and, as I have gotten older, I have learned that I have the right to decline invitations to events that I find overwhelming or where I know I am not going to fit in or enjoy myself.

One advantage to my current workplace is that I have a lot of social interaction with the faculty here, and because it is in a rather structured environment, it is just the right amount of social life for me and not threatening or oppressive. I have also become very bonded with my cat and get a lot of enjoyment out of her closeness and companionship.

Martha's work has been a success on multiple levels and is a good example of how important a good fit is at work. Later in the book, we'll tell you more about her vocational journey and its twists and turns. Her example of continually moving forward in spite of obstacles and a serious setback is inspiring.

I have worked in my current job since 1999. I spend most of my time around science faculty. This is the first job I have had where I am respected for my intellect and skills and not resented or bullied for my quirks. Over the years I have gotten very close to most of the faculty and consider them more as family than as coworkers. I also like the fact that I can manage my time at work independently without a lot of close supervision, and that I can come to work dressed comfortably.

I also appreciate that I work later hours so I don't have to get going too early in the morning. And I appreciate that we have a lot of time off, and that the school year ebbs and flows, so there are busy times which are relieved by quieter times.

COSETTE, 18
College student and aspiring illustrator, currently selling her art on Etsy.com
Diagnosed with Asperger's at age six

Cosette was referred to Debra's practice by her pediatric neurologist for further evaluation and testing. Her assessment confirmed a diagnosis of Asperger's

Disorder. Intelligence testing showed Cosette was very bright—her overall intelligence was in the superior range. It also revealed that she was faster and more accurate at grasping nonverbal concepts, such as shapes and designs, than 99.9% of her peers! Now, on the brink of adulthood, she is using this strength to pursue the avocation of illustrator, and at the age of 18 is already selling some of her work online and at anime and comic con conventions.

Cosette started life with many struggles, and is a great example of a child who needed and benefited greatly from some extra help and guidance. Without the ongoing direct influence and direction of her parents, it's unlikely she would have automatically picked up the skills required for the adolescence she ended up having. It is doubtful she would have been poised for the adulthood that now appears to await her.

Her mother, Stephanie, recalls some of the gut-wrenching beginnings.

> Cosette was like a cat when she was a wee one. She only wanted to be held when she wanted it. She hated to be swaddled. She preferred floor time to lap time. She had tantrums and retreated into a "turtle" position when she was upset. She and I had many problems with defiance and anger. When she started talking, she had echolalia and inappropriate speech. She had horrible sensory problems—everything was too loud, too scratchy, too bright, too everything.
>
> Are you familiar with the *The Miracle Worker*? There is a scene in the movie where Annie and Helen are locked in the dining room while the anxious family hovers outside. Anne finally comes out, disheveled and with egg in her hair, and simply says, "She folded her napkin." We had many days like that when Cosette was young. Getting through the day sometimes was hard for both of us, but we kept "folding the napkin."

Cosette's parents tried many approaches, some more successful than others. Academically, at various points they tried mainstreaming, special education, and even transferring her to a different school. Bullying was a problem. They later found out one of her teachers had been a "yeller" and Cosette had hung in "teeth and toenails" in that noisy class, always exhausted by day's end.

Therapeutically, everything from stickers and charts to PCIT (Parent/Child Interactive Therapy) and social skills groups was tried. Often Cosette outsmarted the adults and was known to pronounce interventions "time wasters."

We did the best we could with the knowledge and resources we had. The most important thing we did was and is to love her unconditionally. I like Cosette. She is an amazing young woman.

Cosette currently attends community college, while also accumulating a portfolio of her artwork and selling drawings at local conventions and her neighborhood used bookstore. You'll read more about the path she took from being a kid in elementary school who liked to draw for her schoolmates, to one that now has her doing commissioned pieces for groups, and most recently, a software company.

DANIEL, 25
Graduate of Brigham Young University, with an M.S. in Math
Diagnosed with Asperger's at age nine

When first interviewed, Daniel was in limbo between graduating and struggling to find employment in his chosen field. After college he had moved back in with his parents, then relocated to a larger town better suited for vocational opportunities. He moved in with his brother, who was already living there. He just learned that he has been invited to participate in training for a position with SAP, a German-owed software company that operates in over 130 countries.

This company specifically looks for employees with autism, with a hiring goal of 2% of their workforce being on the spectrum. Daniel hopes to use his skills in mathematical data analysis, a key component of the corporation's services. Daniel says he was always good at math. His father, John, chuckled as he recalled his son once saying, *"Math is my first language. In fact, I've been doing math my whole life. When I was conceived as a cell, I was already multiplying and dividing!"*

His story is an example of how "it takes a village."

My brother David is good with computers. He inspired me to start teaching myself to program. I was raised Mormon. I was in the Boy Scouts, which is really integrated with our church. Becoming an Eagle Scout is fairly rare, but it was expected. The church had camps where you work on your merit badges and where they don't have Internet— that helped a lot. Later a family friend helped me get a job tutoring.

> When I was in college, my parents talked with my professor once weekly and that helped me stay on task.

Belonging to a close-knit faith community exposed Daniel to many supportive adults who knew him and his family well. John, his father, was his Boy Scout troop leader, and said, "A lot of people knew him since he was born, so they had him figured out." Nancy, his mother, described a rocky journey with others who didn't quite understand her son.

> He did OK in preschool because it was a "parent co-op" setting with just 24 kids, a teacher, and six different parents in the classroom who all knew him. His teacher simply said, "He just marches to a different drummer." But in regular school they weren't flexible and then the real problems started. He's rigid—his teacher can't be rigid too! In sixth grade, the school district talked to his psychologist and placed him at a special education school that worked with children who had been unsuccessful in regular school. The staff there worked with him instead of against him. He stayed three years then transferred to regular high school. He was our fifth child in that school —they'd worked out the bugs with our other kids so they just said, "Tell us what you need!"

Daniel and his family also had the help of professionals, both for diagnosis and treatment. A clinical psychologist evaluated him and then met mostly with Nancy to help her get through difficult challenges throughout the years. Daniel also attended social-relational skills groups where he was able to make friends and progress socially.

When it came time for Daniel to attend college, both parents recommended BYU due to its reputation of expecting high standards both academically and morally, as well as its Accessibility Center. During college, Daniel used their assistance in several ways (which will be detailed later). Upon graduation he also used the resources of the CA Department of Rehabilitation, which his mother Nancy had learned of through a support group for parents of children with autism.

Daniel and both parents realize that challenges remain, primarily in the area of self-motivation and planning. They each commented on how generous their son is, and how he wants to make enough money to donate to charity. They know he'll continue to need support and guidance to reach his goals. His mom credits his siblings with continuing to be a support to him and says, "We're not giving him a choice. He will move forward. We're not giving up."

SARAH, 36
Wildlife Biologist, B.A. in Environmental Science
Diagnosed with Asperger's

Sarah is a good example of how mentors, teachers, and family can nurture special interests that later grow into a productive career.

> My dad loved nature. He shared it with me by taking me on hikes and telling me about the plants we saw. He taught me which ones were edible and how they were used by the Native American culture. Our neighbor, Armida, also taught me to love and value plants. She had a vegetable garden and had me do weeding or other gardening tasks, and then she'd teach me how to cook basic meals with the vegetables. And I had two teachers in middle school who were great influences on me.

Even though Sarah often struggled academically, by focusing on her special interests and by using coping skills she learned from others, she was able to graduate successfully with a degree that has translated into a job she loves.

> My Sunday school teacher, Michele Jones, was a positive influence by teaching me how to be kind to myself as well as to others. She provided structure every Sunday and in addition to being there for patient advice, she also intentionally exposed me to sarcastic humor and jokes and helped me "get" them. This helped me in school when I had to work in groups with other students who naturally communicated in this manner.

Sarah also learned emotional coping skills from observing and interacting with others.

I've struggled with anxiety since I was a child. It's getting better, and I'm able to do my job in spite of it. I've learned to slow down and think about gaining order and control of myself. When I saw the HBO film *Temple Grandin*, I was suddenly relieved of my shame about being different. I used the coping skills shown in the film to help me with my anxiety, my confidence issues, and my sensory sensitivity. I realized that like Temple with her squeeze machine, I wanted a feeling of being held by something predictable and controllable. I use tight jeans and fitted shoes, and I place my hands on my stomach or lower back.

My grandma Barbara used to tickle me on my back when I was a little girl. I found this soothing, and to this day I love massage and its calming effect on me. Grandma also taught me how to be considerate of others and socially appropriate. I used to sing during meals and she put a stop to that. She also taught me to laugh at myself and at my mistakes.

In her job as a wildlife biologist, Sarah is responsible for monitoring wildlife populations and environmental compliance. In addition to childhood influences, she credits her success to more recent mentors as well.

My pathway to getting my first wildlife job was through the back door. My stepmother had an acquaintance, Anne Wallace, who was a wildlife biologist in environmental consulting. I set up an informational interview with her. After that meeting, I sent her an email every month for the next year just to keep in contact. She eventually offered me a short-term job as an independent sub-consultant to her. I did that for only about a month and then her business partner offered me my next job, which was for several months. Later, with this experience, the contacts I had developed, and a reference from Anne, I applied for and was offered a job with a different environmental consulting firm.

Anne was a mentor and has become a friend as well. I appreciate her positivity, kindness, and integrity, which she passed on to me. With her help, I was able to get into my career field, which meant, and means, so much to me.

My autism helps me at work. I am distracted easily, so I am distracted by the presence of every wildlife species moving, sounding, or occurring in my area. This makes detection of wildlife much easier and benefits me in my job of gathering a species list. I have good attention to detail and the ability to do monotonous tasks, like monitoring an animal, for long periods of time. My need to follow rules also helps me because in my job there are many firm rules that must be followed.

I actually met my husband through my work, and he has been my trainer and mentor as well. He has been patient with me, helped me with job contacts, given me wildlife work that was exciting and rewarding, and also helped me refine my social manners.

PATRICK, 26
Aspiring Voice-Over Artist
Diagnosed with Asperger's

Patrick began working with Debra when he was 18 and continued until age 26, when she retired from active practice. He has made great strides in his independence and life skills. From initially spending his days either sleeping or isolated in his room playing video games, he has come full circle and is now pursuing his passion in doing voice-over work, a field that is the direct result of a childhood obsession.

He has had the support of several critical mentors along the way—his parents, his beloved Aunt Mary, his voice coach Cammie Winston, and even a well-known voice-over artist in Hollywood.

His aunt describes him as an infant and toddler:

Even though Patrick was her first son, my sister Ginny knew from the beginning that he responded differently from other infants. He screamed bloody murder at the top of his lungs. Visually, his world seemed to be different, and things that didn't bother others frightened him. He couldn't distinguish between himself and objects. If he spilled milk, he would scream and cry and be angry at the milk. If he fell out of a chair and knocked up against a wall, he would hit the wall and yell, "bad wall!" He was so easily overwhelmed. Once he touched a tree with moss growing on it and went ballistic, screaming and crying. He hated the sensory feeling. I tried to explain the purpose of moss and how it was part of God's natural world. He screamed, "I hate God! Why did he make these things?"

One of Patrick's obsessions as a toddler was watching TV, and he particularly loved commercials and cartoons. He would sit and stare endlessly and soak it all up. What no one realized at the time was that he was memorizing all the voices and actually consciously practicing how to precisely place his tongue and constrict his throat in order to mimic them exactly.

We never discouraged him from making his sounds as long as it was at home, not in public. But that took active intervention on our part. He'd run around the house doing different voices and then would think it was OK to do that in the park or at the grocery store, too. We taught him that the reason it wasn't permitted in the store was that there were other people there, and they were there for a specific reason, and it was not to hear his voices. We never yelled at him; we would explain and redirect him.

Patrick's path to work as a voice-over artist still has its challenges. What is making it possible is a combination of his unique thinking style and abilities, combined with the persistent "push" of those who love him and are finding clever ways of creating opportunities for him.

Along the way, Patrick has obtained his driver's license, taken improvisation classes, used his vocal talent as a volunteer to record books for the Society for the Blind, and broadened his horizons in many areas ranging from diet to travel. You'll learn more about the specific steps and the people who have helped keep him moving in the right direction in the following chapters.

*Patrick's early special interest in sounds
first took the form of "voicing" his toys.*

CHAPTER 2

The Three Necessary Components of Your Child's Success

1. Avoiding Learned Helplessness
2. Learning Optimism and Resisting Habitual Negative Thinking
3. The Critical Impact of Mentors

Whether you think you can, or think you can't, you're probably right.

—*Henry Ford*

A mentor is someone who allows you to see the hope inside yourself.

—*Oprah Winfrey*

E ach of the people whose stories you just read encountered unique challenges and struggles. Yet they found strategies and support that helped them move on and create meaningful, productive lives. We're going to give you examples of how they did it.

A recurring theme in each of the stories was that every person kept moving forward even in the face of obstacles. They discovered how to stay positive enough to continue to develop. They didn't give in to their doubts, and they didn't quit when they hit obstacles.

Others were often there to help them, making sure they didn't withdraw into isolation, inactivity, or helplessness. Family members and others supported them in staying hopeful and finding opportunities. Also, every single person profiled mentioned at least one adult who exposed him or her to new ideas, to new ways of thinking about themselves, and to novel experiences. These components helped pave the way to each person's success.

They weren't a coddled group of kids. Their parents were all unique—some were absent, some were struggling just to provide, and some were handling large families with their share of crisis points. One common denominator was that each person profiled was encouraged and "stretched" just outside their comfort zone by at least one adult in their life. This helped keep them positive and prevented them from falling into chronic learned helplessness, a condition that is frequently embedded in autistic kids and which we'll introduce you to in this chapter.

Start by Creating a Positive Mindset

Always praise your child's tangible actions. Generalities can be confusing or unusable by those on the autism spectrum. So when you say, "You're such a great kid," or "You can do anything you set your mind to," these are well intended, but will not be as effective as a specific reference. Instead say, "You did a great job fixing dinner tonight. I know you were nervous and weren't sure you could do it. But you followed the recipe carefully and it turned out delicious." People with autism typically can't organize a response to a generalized comment or an open-ended question about their goals.

When you praise qualities of their personality, be equally specific. Avoid generalities like "You are a kind person." Instead, give your child a concrete example of their kindness: "I was happy to see you help your father mow the lawn. You know he's been working extra hours and has been tired. That was really considerate and kind of you."

Self-esteem and the courage to try new things come gradually to many of our children, and they are often their own worst critics. They have frequently felt different at best, and been mercilessly bullied at worst. Many have integrated a negative self-image, and we have to actively help them reverse this.

Jaime says he still regrets how he let bullies influence his self-perception.

I should have separated myself from them. But it was confusing because the bullies would sometimes be nice to me in one-on-one situations. But whenever anyone else was around, they'd default to treating me poorly. My mistake was allowing them the opportunity to continue pestering me, and letting them assert authority over me. My mistake was placing even the slightest value on the opinions of those that treated me badly.

Avoiding Learned Helplessness

Many children on the autism spectrum are casualties of what is called "learned helplessness," and this must be dealt with head-on. This term was coined by psychologist Martin Seligman, best known for his work in the field of "positive psychology." Knowing the basics of his research will help you help your child. Dr. Seligman discovered that when animals or people are repeatedly subjected to negative environments that they can't control, they pretty quickly give up. But the really scary thing he observed was that *even when circumstances change and become positive*, they still act powerless!

In one classic study, he placed three groups of dogs in a room with a floor that emitted a mild shock—not enough to harm the dogs, but unpleasant enough that they would naturally want to escape it. The first dogs (Group #1) experienced the shock, and were then released. Two other sets of dogs (Group #2 and #3) were yoked together in pairs. Each dog in the pair had a lever they could press with their paw. The levers actually worked for Group #2—when the dog pressed it, the shock stopped. But the dogs in Group #3 had sham levers—they didn't do a thing.

The dogs in the first and second group quickly recovered from the experience, but the dogs with useless levers began to exhibit signs of chronic depression. And most frightening, when they were later put in a similar situation, they generalized their powerlessness and acted completely helpless.

They were put in a room with a low partition. The floor gave them a mild shock. They weren't in a harness this time—they could have easily jumped over the partition and escaped it. But instead they simply lay down passively and whined. They didn't even try.

Without our help, our children are like these dogs. They are very vulnerable to giving up. Kids on the autism spectrum are especially susceptible to learned helplessness for several reasons. First, they often have a history of emotional trauma. This may surprise you. But being subject to the sudden onset of sensory overload "storms" and the emotional tornados we call meltdowns is traumatic. And being bullied, which almost all children on the spectrum have endured, is definitely traumatic.

They also give up quickly due to their neurological wiring. It is difficult for them to see the big picture. In fancy terminology this is called lacking "central coherence." Non-autistic people naturally look for the "big (central, coherent) picture" and process information within that context. Autistic children rarely do. Instead, they hyper-focus on one part of their experience and fail to see alternative choices or options.

Parents and therapists have to intentionally and consistently counteract this. With young kids, you tell them explicitly what alternatives are available. With older kids and teens, you help them come up with their own choices. Once they figure out an alternative and can put it in words, you have to make sure they act on it as soon as possible in order to reinforce it.

An Example from Temple

Temple met a woman after speaking at a conference in Argentina. The woman shared that she was afraid to go into certain stores, so she was really limited in her shopping. This distressed and inconvenienced her and she wanted to overcome it. Temple let the woman briefly talk, and then moved into action mode.

There was a newspaper stand nearby and the woman was interested in knowing the day's news. Temple stood aside and told the woman to walk up and buy a newspaper. She did it successfully. Temple congratulated her. Then she confronted her distorted thinking by pointing out that her self-limiting thinking was inaccurate, because she had just proved she was in fact able to make a purchase at a new place. If Temple had just listened or gotten into a prolonged conversation about the woman's fears, the woman probably would just have gotten more anxious. She certainly wouldn't have initiated a purchase herself. Sometimes we have to "strike while the iron is hot." It was a teachable moment that Temple grabbed. Parents can do the same.

Another Example: Patrick Learns to Enjoy Eating Out

Patrick's Aunt Mary gives another good example of taking concrete action and using a person's desire to overcome their fear.

> Patrick used to be afraid to go to restaurants. But he loved to eat. So I would take him out even when he was being resistant. We would go to simple places that often had menus on the wall, but even this was overwhelming. At first he acted helpless and would cry and say, "I'm not going to eat!" He used to freeze and refuse to make a decision. I would tell him that while there is no rush, you can, and must decide.
>
> "Search your brain," I would say. I would bring him back up to the counter (he'd inevitably have walked away by then), and we would practice breathing and choosing an option. I would also have him see the big picture by paying attention to other people in the restaurant and their conversations so that he broke out of his tunnel vision.

In summary, she says, "Always teach about ways to get past the anxiety and helplessness rather than let it take over the situation."

These days one of Patrick's favorite things to do with his aunt is going out to eat. She tells him he has become a "restaurant social butterfly." She recalls the day she watched him come out of the restroom laughing and joking with a woman in the waiting area. "I was so proud of him!"

From his own perspective, Patrick says, "Mary used to take me out to restaurants and I just didn't know what to order. If it's a place you order from a waiter, I still tend to ask for recommendations. That makes it easier. But it's also helped me branch out and try new foods I would never try as a kid and didn't even know existed!"

Patrick was asked for some examples of the most "exotic" foods he's tried and liked. The joy in his voice came through when he described them.

> Dim sum and blue cheese and feta cheese. Salmon was my "gateway" food! I thought, oh my God—this is delicious!" I get kind of crazy around salmon! And there are so many types of fish out there!

Patrick's Aunt Mary instinctively did the two things that Dr. Seligman found works to reverse learned helplessness. With the dogs, he had to put them back in the old situation and then he physically manipulated them over the barrier. He literally lifted them and moved their legs in ways that mimicked how the dog would naturally jump. This is what Mary did when she went and got Patrick and brought him back up to the menu.

But there is a second necessary step. If the dogs were lifted over the barrier just once or even only a few times, it didn't work. They retreated to helplessness. Dr. Seligman had to repeat the physical action over and over. But the dogs finally got it and the effect lasted! Same with Patrick—it took lots of restaurant trips, but now he looks forward to going out to eat.

Learning Optimism and Resisting Habitual Negative Thinking

Dr. Seligman also coined a second term: "learned optimism." Based on earlier work of both Albert Ellis's rational emotive behavior therapy (REBT) and Aaron Beck's cognitive behavior therapy (CBT), Seligman added two more pieces. In both of these therapies, it is assumed that something activates an event (A), then we respond with a rational or irrational belief (B), and then this belief influences the consequence (C). When we get stuck in irrational beliefs, we get stuck in self-defeating consequences.

Seligman realized that more than intellectual insight is needed to maintain changes in our behavior, so he added "disputation" (D) and "energization" (E) to the model. Disputation means we have to *expose our kids to counter-evidence of their beliefs*—often in the midst of their vigorous resistance. Energization means we *actively celebrate the success that follows making positive choices and reclaiming autonomy.*

These two steps to change bad habits are particularly important for ASD kids. Autistic kids have brains that are built to be great at focusing like an intense laser. But the downside is their brains don't naturally try on alternative perspectives or explanations. We have to guide them in this direction, and we have to have them practice it *over and over*. When autistic kids get stuck on an irrational belief, they're unlikely to unstick themselves without our active intervention and help. We have to provide them both insight *and* action.

The insight must be based on clear logic, not an appeal to emotion. And even then, as Ellis famously said, "insight alone will help you very little." Our kids need specific ways to recognize their thinking distortions and concrete ways to shift that thinking. Below are three ideas that are easy to understand and can help you guide your child.

Know the Three "Ps" on the Road to Success

There are three easy ways to remember how to teach our kids to resist habitual negative thinking and self-blame. Known as the "3 Ps," they involve concepts of Permanence, Pervasiveness, and Personalization. We'll describe how each one can be used to help people on the spectrum.

"Permanence"

Our kids often assume that bad events are permanent and good events are temporary. They aren't necessarily consciously aware of this belief. It needs to be clearly pointed out to them—over and over. And they need specific examples of bad things they've experienced that in fact were not permanent.

Debra remembers working with Patrick when he was learning to drive. After a year of practicing in parking lots and side streets, then taking driver's education classes, he signed up for the on-road examination. He failed it (as he was convinced he would, in spite of evidence to the contrary that he was capable of good, safe driving). His mind was saying he would fail, his anxiety skyrocketed, and he made a mistake he didn't make in practice.

After this "bad" event, Patrick swore he'd *never* again try to take the test. He was adamant! He believed that *if he failed once he would always fail*. He retreated into helplessness. As his Aunt Mary says, "He needs more than average success before he'll own it, and even then he struggles because his negative voice is still loud."

It took some time for Patrick's emotional state to return to baseline, and then we had many talks about the faulty logic in his thinking. It also took him getting back in the driver's seat as soon as possible. We renewed our emphasis on relaxation and breathing technique and rehearsed self-talk. He retook the exam and passed. He now drives both locally and out of town! Now when other "bad" things happen, this example serves to remind him that while his initial belief may always be "once a bad outcome, always a bad outcome," this in fact is untrue. He has indisputable proof.

Patrick and his Dad—a successful outcome!

"Pervasiveness"

A second self-defeating attitude—"pervasiveness"—is assuming that difficulty or failure in one area means life *as a whole* is a failure. Optimistic people compartmentalize problems, but ASD children need extra and specific help with this. When they have difficulty with one task, kids on the spectrum often conclude they are bad at every task. They'll need your help listing areas they are good at. Better yet, get them involved as soon as possible in an activity they feel good about. Keep up involvement in that area on a regular basis so that they routinely experience mastery. It doesn't have to be a big deal thing. Sarah, the wildlife biologist profiled earlier, remembers how important it was to help her neighbor Armida with small tasks such as weeding alongside her in the garden. It's hard to mess up weeding, and Armida was genuinely appreciative of the help.

"Personalization"

The last "P" is personalization. There is a huge difference between how optimists and pessimists attribute cause to events. When bad things happen, pessimists assume they personally caused it. Optimists assume it was just bad luck or bad circumstances. On the other hand, when good things happen, pessimists assume it was just "dumb luck." Optimists, however, internalize a sense of achievement and give themselves credit for their role in success.

Katie, the mom of Scott, the former quality assurance tester, recalled a game she created to motivate and reward learning manners. This is a great example of one simple way to both reinforce specific skills and internalize a child's sense of personal accomplishment. Scott's mom made up "the manners game," which was played at the dinner table at least once every week.

I'd place two nickels in front of each person's place setting. Then I'd pick one table manner I wanted to teach—one week not chewing with your mouth open, another not putting your elbows on the table, and so forth. I made it a fun game and my husband and I played along, even making mistakes on purpose to give Scott and his siblings a chance to spot them. Every time a child spotted a mistake, they were awarded one of the nickels belonging to the person who made the mistake. They got to keep it and save or spend it. But if they made a mistake, they lost a nickel and there was no arguing or whining allowed. The kids found the game very motivating and didn't realize they were learning rules and attitudes—they just liked the treat of having game night.

The Critical Impact of Mentors

A very important ingredient in every personal profile in Chapter 1 was that each individual had at least one parent, teacher, neighbor, employer, or other mentor to guide them. These adults blended being a positive role model, a source of advice or information, and someone who expected effort and accountability.

These folks weren't professionals and they didn't necessarily know about autism, but they recognized the uniqueness of each child and sensed their areas of need. They created opportunities to both nurture and instruct the child. They saw the best in each youngster, even when that child couldn't see it for themselves. And when the child felt that appreciation, it stayed in their hearts forever.

Listening to the stories of those who were profiled, it was really obvious how fondly they remembered their mentors. Some stayed in touch with them for many years. It was clear that even those who have lost touch treasure the memories of their time together. Interviews with mentors were also often powerful and moving. More than one mentor shed tears as they told their stories and then heard how important they had been.

Mentors Who Were Friends or Teachers

Martha, the science department clerk now in her 50s, talked about a nurturing mentor she first met as a little girl. She stayed in contact with her even into her college years.

> When I was little, my father's woman friend Mary took a lot of interest in me. She helped me feel loved when I was not getting that at home. She provided me an ear for my sorrows about my upbringing, about bullying at home and school, and about my loneliness. My mother had died when I was three, and my father and his mother raised me. Mary was the only person who made me feel like I was a special and unique person. When I went to college, I lived close enough to her to visit on weekends. I graduated with a bachelor's degree in economics and was an excellent student. But I was bullied throughout, so Mary was a welcome respite. I always felt safe with her.

Several mentors were teachers. These educators seemed to combine passion for their avocation, commitment to the student, and a creative approach to matching each child's unique mind to the subject matter at hand.

Sarah, now 36 and a wildlife biologist, was eager to talk about Mr. Shanks, her middle school ecology teacher, and Mrs. Letsos, her middle school math teacher.

> Mr. Shanks reinforced my budding love of nature! His positive influence encouraged my creativity. He was always enthusiastic and appreciative of me. He exposed me to ideas about ecology and also, like my father, to Native American ideas. My math teacher, Mrs. Letsos, recognized and used my growing interests in nature to help me learn. She applied math functions to shapes found in plants and animals,

which was by now something I loved. So she always had my attention in class!

Cosette, who recently graduated from high school, remembers how important her sixth grade teacher was to both her and her classmates.

Mrs. Warner was the teacher that understood my autism the best. Before her, most other teachers could scarcely believe that I had autism. That's because I seemed to function perfectly most of the time and I was very smart. But my behavior was erratic, and I had terrible fits of anxiety and outbursts of strong emotion. Mrs. Warner not only believed me, she also educated the other kids about what I had. After that the kids didn't try to bully me or mock me for my erratic behavior like I had experienced in earlier elementary school grades. Now they were on my side and supported me through my sixth grade year.

The Mathematics of Plants—Making Science Relevant to a Student

Sarah's science teacher, Mrs. Marilyn Letsos, has a love and appreciation of how math intersects with the natural world. Her passion was immediately evident in talking with her. She eagerly yet patiently described how nature's spirals, such as snail shells and sunflower blooms, follow a mathematical principle known as the Fibonacci sequence, adding, *"Nature is so full of wonderful mathematical phenomena. There are lots of geometric shapes in nature."*

Mrs. Letsos also recognized the value of having her students do more than listen. She had them physically experience math, which is vital for visual thinkers on the autism spectrum.

To teach how the tilt of the earth causes the seasons, I would have the students actually go out and check the time the sun came up and what time it set each day. Then they would measure how much it changed from day to day. I'd also have them go outside and measure the shadows of things such as trees and tall buildings. This taught them angles and geometry.

She had a natural appreciation for the challenges some students faced in math class. She related that she herself "hated" math as a child. On her classroom wall she displayed a large poster picturing Albert Einstein and his quote, "Do not worry if you have problems with mathematics. I can assure you mine are much worse." Perhaps most importantly, this was a teacher who valued each child's uniqueness and whose goal was to help students reach their individual potential.

As a child myself, I didn't "get it" the way math was presented. But as a middle school teacher, I had to teach it! Once I started teaching it, I loved it. I loved it because it was actually fun and interesting! I realized that there are many valid ways to approach and solve a problem, and I could see how important it is to validate my students' thinking —especially if it was original—even if it didn't match the approach given in the textbook.

I would give them some sort of puzzle they had to work out in small groups. Each student would approach the problem differently, and that made it even more powerful because they could see how a problem can be solved in more than one way. They could also see how important their contribution was to the process, even if they didn't come up with the final solution.

Every one of our brains is unique and works differently. But they can all make valuable contributions and we need them all! I tried to foster a personal sense of confidence and appreciation, in each child, for their own thinking process and sense of logic. My deep desire was to make their education a tool of empowerment. Otherwise, we don't have any business keeping them in school unless it serves their self-realization. Then they can serve others and become truly orderly, productive, contributing members of society.

Getting Families and Schools to Work Together

It does take a village. If your child does not have a special "mentor" teacher, make sure you approach the school and ask for help preparing your child for adulthood. If you do not have an IEP this is much harder, so that is your first step. Once you have an IEP, generally provided under the category of "Other Health Impaired" (versus intellectual disability), then you as the parent must take the lead and be sure formal transition planning is included. This must spell out how your child will get vocational training in the form of both job skill instruction and on-the-job internships prior to graduation.

Researchers have shown that families working with schools produce the best outcome for ASD youth. Most schools don't have formal programs, so you have to create your own. The vast majority of schools will tell you they don't have these sorts of programs. Keep going up the chain of command to the school district. Go online for help and advice. Many of the autism advocacy groups have information on getting these resources, and another good website is wrightslaw.com, a site devoted to special education law and advocacy.

All ASD youth in high school should be preparing for life after graduation before graduation. Detailed steps should be written into their IEP by their junior year.

One study found many advantages when at least one parent and the student are directly involved with the school's planning, and those who started one year earlier showed significant benefits. These students and their parents reported significantly higher expectations for the future, and the students had a higher sense of self-determination and a better sense of vocational decision-making ability.

One student cited in the study, Daniel, identified a goal of working in the film industry and attending college to study film or broadcasting. His planning team helped him research occupations and job requirements in the film industry, and people and organizations in his community where he could gain experience. Daniel's planning facilitator developed an internship opportunity at the public access channel in his community. The student's school provided an aide to support the internship, and Daniel was able to learn skills related to operating professional video cameras, lighting, and sound. In addition, Daniel was supported to write a movie review column for his school newspaper. Through these experiences, he became more aware of what he did and did not like, what supports he required to be successful, and how to communicate his needs to others. As Daniel's mother noted, "He is able to dream, and explore opportunities, and nothing is going to hold him back."

Mentors Can Even be Media Personalities or Superheroes

Several individuals also mentioned role models that served as inspiration and comfort, even though they didn't know them personally. Some sources of security and identity were celebrities or cartoon characters.

Jaime, who now works for one of the world's largest technology companies, had examples from both categories.

> I was already the outcast by elementary school. I remember liking Gonzo on the *Muppet Babies,* whose alien race was self-professed "Weirdo." He ignored what others thought. He was in love with Miss Piggy and was artistic and brainy—just being himself and not trying to be anything else. He was honest and good, but not perfect, and I could relate to that.
>
> In high school, I loved Spider-Man. To me he was the most relatable superhero. He didn't live in a mansion and he had difficulty maintaining relationships, despite his great power and even greater intellect. He was noble and really smart and very funny.
>
> I also found that one way I handled teasing from others was I modeled myself on aspects of Conan O'Brien (an American television host, comedian, writer, and voice actor). I like those who approach almost all subjects with absurdity. I watched his show and observed that Conan's sense of humor is to be self-deprecating. It is far more difficult for others to make fun of one if one is already doing so. It is quite disarming to them, yet also appealing. That helped me.

CHAPTER 3

How to Break Your Child's
Bad Habits—
A Necessary Step So Your Child
Keeps Moving Forward

Limits, like fear, are often an illusion.

—*Michael Jordan*

Hope is a function of struggle.

—*Brené Brown, Ph.D.*

It's excruciating to watch your child experience emotional distress. Your natural instinct is to do whatever it takes to protect them from pain. Doubtless you've had plenty of practice doing the "rescue dance." You grabbed them by the back of the shirt when as toddlers they yet again darted away from you to God knows what stranger or danger. Later you made "apology eyes" at waitresses/clerks/other moms as you rushed them out of the restaurant/store/party when they started to meltdown and scream the way only an autistic child can scream. And now, as they have grown older, you may find yourself turning away and backing off when they slam shut their bedroom door for the zillionth time if you inadvertently interrupt their never-ending video game.

These behaviors became habits. When your child was younger, they really did need you to be their proxy in a dangerous world. They relied on you to spot danger they were oblivious to, to speak up for them when they couldn't find words, and to retreat instead of moving closer when they reached overload and couldn't handle what would have been comfort to another child.

Now it's time to break these habits. They no longer serve you or them. Your child is growing up, and they need to develop as much self-sufficiency as they are capable of. If you take on tasks your child is actually able to handle on their own, you inadvertently elicit feelings of ineptness and impotence. Trying to help when it's not genuinely needed creates a sense of incompetency. Your child instead desperately needs (even if it comes with kicking and screaming) a sense of self-agency. This comes from handling tough situations as independently as possible.

The Teenage Years are Different for ASD Teens

If you have neurotypical children, you may marvel at how differently they navigated their teenage years compared to your child on the autism spectrum. It often seems like adolescence really never registers as a separate developmental phase for a spectrum child. They may enter into their teens seemingly unchanged. They might continue to pursue the same special interests and are usually content to entertain themselves in isolation. They prefer to stay home rather than joining their NT peers, who are now yearning to get out of the house and explore the world. You probably don't have to worry about them drinking and driving, but it may seem like you're going to be stuck chauffeuring them for life, since many have no apparent interest in getting a driver's license.

This might not exactly describe your child, but you probably related to at least some of these common themes. Adolescence for teens on the spectrum usually has a very different tone and set of struggles than for neurotypical teens. While NTs are chomping at the bit for freedom from their parents, taking increasingly bold (exciting to them, nerve-racking to you) risks, and spending proportionally much more time with peers than with family, this isn't the case for the typical spectrum child.

Instead, they may be retreating further into themselves. While their peers hunger for driver's licenses, engage in sexual and drug experimentation, wear the hippest fashions, and attend parties, kids on the spectrum often don't care about these things. More commonly, they actively disdain these urges. Yet you suspect that under their contempt and antipathy they may actually be lonelier than ever. And you're probably right.

If your teen has no interest in typical adolescent pursuits, don't sweat it. Autistic teenagers can sometimes basically skip traditional adolescence. Successful autistic adults often became involved in "adult" pursuits while their peers were busy fine-tuning socializing with each other. Socializing with teenagers is not a necessary life skill! As long as your child is active and engaged with *someone* (versus being reclusive or apathetic), it's fine for them to hang out with adults instead of their peers. It won't make them popular at school, but who cares? A successful life is not about popularity.

Teens Need Straight Talk

If you haven't talked to your teen openly about their diagnosis, do it now. Hopefully you're way past this point on the journey, but we realize there may be some readers who suspect their teen is on the spectrum, but haven't yet received a diagnosis or brought it up. We can't stress enough how strongly we believe that knowledge will serve you better than guessing. Your child already knows they are different, and they've certainly come up with their own explanation for that difference. Without accurate information and feedback, sadly they've most likely explained their differences to themselves in ways that are judgmental and demoralizing.

If you haven't yet broached the subject of autism, you can start by providing brief written information. If you know there's no way they'll read anything, try just "happening" to be watching a YouTube video of a teen on the spectrum when you know they'll be walking by (there are scores of really good ones online these days—use the YouTube search feature). Or do an online search and print out a self-diagnosis quiz or checklist from the Internet. Put it in their room. We are *not* suggesting that online screening questionnaires are sufficient for accurate diagnosis. They can, however, help provide an easy way to ease into a discussion.

Don't be afraid to give them other books as well. When Temple was 15 years old, her Aunt Anne handed her a copy of Norman Vincent Peale's *The Power of Positive Thinking* with instructions to read it. It made an impression that resulted in changes in her thinking and attitude.

Without repeated and vigorous loving pushes from you, your teen on the spectrum may continue living the life of an adolescent, forever frozen in time. They may be perfectly content letting you handle all the necessary tasks of daily life. For example, they may not see the need for driving, as they don't have a vision that includes going to new places.

Living in Their Bedroom is Not an Acceptable Life

Neurotypical teens usually fantasize about their first apartment and yearn for the freedom it symbolizes. Your spectrum teen may instead prefer to keep everything the same—staying at home in their own bedroom, even with their old, childhood furniture. You know this is not healthy, but they may see no disadvantages to it. So it is up to you to make sure this doesn't happen. Because left to their own devices, many of them will not make any plans for moving out and moving on.

Temple recalls old Mr. Patey, the headmaster at her boarding school, and how he would not allow her to become a recluse in her room. She looks back and realizes how wise he was. When she didn't want to go to the regular Friday night movie at school, he told her she had two choices; She could either run the projector or sit in the audience, but she could not stay in her room.

She also had to show up at every meal. We think your child should, too. Eating in their bedroom has become a bad habit for some kids, and parents ignore it or even take food to them. You will help your child if you insist they come to the dinner table—not just to eat, but also to participate in conversation and in setting and clearing the table. Our world has gotten so busy that regular Sunday family dinners seem to be a thing of the past. That's unfortunate, because they were a great opportunity for kids to learn manners and how to interact with extended family that often joined in.

Many Spectrum Kids are Afraid When They Hit Adolescence

Hopefully you've already taught your child a variety of living skills that have increased their competencies and overall maturity. But many lag behind their peers. Reaching adolescence brings new challenges. The teen and young adult years require a developmental stretch that is bigger than any they've faced so far. Children on the spectrum commonly fear change in general, and even if they don't voice it, this heightens, and they are often profoundly afraid during adolescence. Few are confident they'll make it as adults. They would prefer that you allow them to continue as children, playing the protective parent role just like you always have.

If your child is genuinely incapable of independently navigating adulthood due to more severe cognitive or physical limitations or mental illness, then of course you plan accordingly with appropriate support and modifications. But we are seeing too many teens and their families on the higher end of the autism spectrum mistaking challenges for incapacitating limitations. We cringe when some parents seem to assume that even their children of average or superior intelligence will spend their adult lives on disability funding. Our experience has been that most of these teens, with guidance, can shift into adult lives of successful employment and independent living.

Yet we are finding that many teens are dragging their feet. They are too comfortable with the status quo, and too nervous about the unknown. They desperately need your help. They need you to have faith in them even when they have none. They need you to transform your role of protector into that of encouraging advocate, champion, and loving pusher.

If you're extremely lucky, your teen on the spectrum will self-initiate moving forward into new adult territory. But if they were showing signs of doing that, you probably wouldn't have picked up or needed this book. So let's assume your child is more typical—they are going to move forward only when you are behind them pushing! And they probably won't go willingly—not ones to "lean in," they may twist and turn and sag backwards like a dead weight!

This is a critical juncture in your child's journey. Just when they are upping their resistance, we're asking you to increase your offensive push. We could try to pretty it up and say "you'll do fine" and "it's not that bad." But if you haven't prepared for this period with a history of loving pushes, let's face it—this may be a daunting stage. In truth, even if you've always worked hard to keep your child developing and maturing, this particular crossroads brings new challenges.

Why These New Challenges are a GOOD Sign and Part of Hope

In her book *Daring Greatly*, popular author and speaker Brené Brown writes that in her travels across the country she has found a growing concern on the part of parents and teachers that children are not learning to handle adversity or disappointment. She believes this is because we are always rescuing and protecting them. She points out that the concerned parents worried about their lagging teens are the same ones who are chronically intervening in their children's lives. While she doesn't specifically address autism, her thoughts about how parents inadvertently sabotage their children's emotional growth are particularly relevant for children on the spectrum.

She points out that the impact of rescuing and intervening can range from unhelpful to downright dangerous. Why? Because depriving our children of the opportunity to struggle or even fail, and then recover, robs them of learning hope. We tend to think of hope as an emotion based on faith. We think of it as the feeling that "things will turn out for the best," based in part on confidence and trust. It implies more of an attitude of calm determinism rather than an active, industrious stance.

But there is a large body of research on hope that shows it is *not* an emotion— it's a specific way of thinking. It is an attitude that leads to concrete action. Emotions may play a supporting role, but they're not the main source of the motivation behind hope. The backbone of the motivation is a mindset that leads directly to planning, exertion, and execution. And that inevitably involves struggle.

An Example—Patrick's Father Demonstrates the Importance of Struggle

Patrick's father wanted to impart the value of learning a healthy view of struggling, and making "mistakes," and how to keep the faith when that happens.

I took Patrick to work with me. I'm a contractor. Contractors make mistakes and we fix them. So while he was there I was using a drill to put in a door lock and the drill busted out the other side. So I had to repair the door. Or you might hit a grain in the wood and the drill goes the wrong way and there goes your drill. It happens. So then you fix it.

He has this idea that I do everything perfectly—that other people don't make mistakes and it's always easy for them. I wanted him to see that's bunk.

I want him to know we all struggle along the way. When I started in this work, my first job was sweeping. Then I dug holes. Then I carried lumber. Then they gave me a hammer. And now, 35 years later, I have people under me who sweep and carry and dig. No one starts at the top. He has this fear that if he gets a job and doesn't know how to do it, something awful will happen. I tell him 'they teach you'—if you get a job making sandwiches they show you their way of doing it.

Your job is to remember and do it right. He's too stuck on being embarrassed or a failure.

Your Child Needs Extra Help to Build Hope

Let us introduce you to "Hope Theory," because it has major valuable lessons for parents raising children with challenges. Psychologist Charles Snyder was another researcher fascinated by the concept of hope and how it affects our health, work, education, and personal meaning. He outlined two pathways to hope.

First, he said hope is built on setting realistic goals. Our kids on the spectrum need help with this step. Ideas from parents, teachers, and other mentors are critical. If our kids aren't exposed to various career options, experiences, and possibilities, they can't have any realistic goals. With no exposure to feasible occupations, they are more likely to restrict their goals to unrealistic ones like becoming game designers, even though they don't have any skills in that area other than playing video games.

Second, we have to help our kids figure out how to go about achieving those goals. This is often a tricky step for those with autism. Because they're often predisposed to inflexible thinking, and rarely develop alternatives on their own, they need a great deal of outside help in this area. Again, parents and others must take the lead or it won't happen. You have to take your kid out into the world and show them lots of different educational and work environments. Take them to your local community college and schedule a meeting with the disability office or one of the counselors. Walk the campus. Go to the bookstore. Show them a course catalogue. Arrange tours of companies in your area. Get brief meetings with people who work in fields that are even remotely interesting to your kid.

Even with exposure, most people aren't going to try things if they don't see the point. If an activity doesn't naturally attract your child, they're certainly not going to do it unless they can start to see that it's a means to a goal. For our autistic youth, the goal really has to be spelled out. Connect the dots for them. It may be obvious to you, but it probably won't even occur to them.

Kids Will Try Something New If You Can Link It to Their Goal: 3 Examples from Temple

Temple remembers doing many things she hated only because they were means to a goal she cared about. For example, in order to graduate she had to take English literature. She was certain she would HATE that class! Turns out she loved it. She would never have been exposed to it, and would never realized she loved it, if it hadn't been an absolute requirement.

She also remembers being afraid to go to the store by herself. She was building something and needed a piece of lumber, but she didn't want to go to the lumber-yard alone. Her mother wisely knew that her building project was a reflection of a strong special interest, so she used that as leverage. She refused to go with Temple, because she was pretty sure she could manage it by herself and that her motivation to finish the project would override her anxiety and reluctance. She was right. Temple wanted that board and she managed to get herself to the store, make the purchase without her mother's help, and come home to finish her design.

Temple also remembers that when she was younger she didn't take care of her hygiene or appearance. However, she wanted a job at a feedlot. She couldn't reach her goal, which was related to her special interests, unless she cleaned up. This was made clear to her in no uncertain terms. That was the "hook" that got her to improve her cleanliness. Now cleanliness is a habit and routine. She can still choose her own unique Western clothing—your child can be eccentric and still make it in the world—but she operates within the bounds of acceptable appearance for her particular work. This is a great example of how your child has to have a reason for changing their behavior. And it has to be a real reason, based on logic and preferably linked directly to a special interest.

Magic Happens When You Introduce New Things

We hope you're convinced by now that many of the activities necessary for our children to reach success have to be introduced by parents or others. Only then can that magical transformation happen—when something they expect to "hate" or be bored by turns into something enjoyable and stimulating. It can even turn into a new special interest that can lead to a career.

Few of us achieve goals via a straight, smooth path. We encounter unexpected and frustrating obstacles along the way. We might even discover that our original goal was misguided and not a practical or good fit. We have to retreat, rethink, and revise our plan. We might need to make major changes, even though we're tired and disheartened. We have to sustain belief in ourselves during this period of ambiguity and keep moving forward in spite of our uncertainly.

This is *very* difficult for the autistic brain, because its neural pathways are highly focused and deeply channeled. Shifting course can be literally painful. When a goal is stymied, most autistic children and teens "freeze." Not only do their brains fail to automatically search for alternative pathways to their goal, but they often become overwhelmed both emotionally and cognitively. Unless they have previously acquired the skills necessary to stop this cascade of negativity and fear, they will be engulfed by it. (Martha's and Patrick's stories below are good examples.) Depression and anxiety may set in or worsen. Their natural tendency is to retreat and/or announce they will never try again because they will never succeed. Your heart sinks, and it feels like one step forward just met two steps back.

As a parent or professional, this is when you may experience empathy for their genuinely miserable state, as well as impatience and irritation. When you're disappointed or afraid for your child, you have to hold those emotions in check. Instead, you must remind yourself that this is a classic part of the journey, not its endpoint.

First, calmly listen to your child's fears or ranting without yet offering solutions or trying to fix it. Gently ask questions to get a fuller sense of their particular negative self-beliefs that have kicked in. Has this convinced them that they are worthless? That the world is out to get them? That they are never going to succeed?

They need some time for their emotional arousal to diminish. The chemicals that are now coursing through their brain and fueling fear and negativity will likely decline over time. This may take days, not hours. In the meantime, keep a regular schedule, offer small acts of kindness, and simply voice that you can see their level of distress and you realize it feels awful. Unless you see signs that they are open to talking or listening, though, just give them some space for now, knowing you will return to the issue soon.

Let Them Rebound and Grow

If you succumb to your own fear at this point – by either arguing or letting your child give up—you have reinforced their reaction and *you have sabotaged hope*. Since hope is not an automatic emotion, but a learned behavior, we have the opportunity to foster it by our own behaviors. Brené Brown also stresses that to teach our kids how to think and act in a hopeful manner, we have to provide relationships characterized by boundaries, consistency, and support. Stay strong; don't let your child's fears and setbacks detract from continuing to plan and take action. Regroup but keep going.

For example, if your child tries their first job and gets fired, they may insist that they will get fired from every job and it's not worth trying again. Let them talk about this without much initial response from you other than calm questions that help them identify how they reached their conclusions. Give them a day or two to mope, but tell them you are having a family meeting in a few days to brainstorm how to keep moving forward.

Find out why they were fired—don't take their word for it. Call or meet with their supervisor, with your child listening in and contributing via speakerphone, or accompanying you. Don't do everything for your child, but be there to guide them. If your child was fired because of a job or social skill deficit, work on it. Set specific goals so you can measure success (Chapter 5 will show you how to use standard therapeutic approaches with your child if they don't have a therapist).

Remember that children or adults with high levels of hopefulness have been through adversity. Hope does not spring from contentment or security. The house of hope is built brick by brick—calamity upon hardship upon mishap upon mistake. With each trial, our children have the opportunity to develop their resilience, skills, flexibility, and adaptability. These trials provide necessary occasions to struggle and grow. And in doing that, they learn how to believe in themselves.

Real Life Example #1: Patrick's Journey Gaining Confidence and Learning Voice-Over Skills

Both Patrick and Cammie, his voiceover coach, had insights into how important it is to keeping moving forward even when struggling. This story illustrates the concept of hope as a way of thinking, and how we can creatively come up with options for our kids even when they think they can't do something.

> Cammie gives me just the right level of persistence. If anyone pushes me too hard, I shut down. That usually happens in general—too much and I give up. If something is not "too hard" but still uncomfortable, I'll sort of feel like "this is ridiculous"—both the hard thing some-

one wants me to do, plus how I am feeling about it. I definitely have self-awareness now when I'm resisting. But at least for now, I still need someone else to push me past it.

Cammie recalls her thoughts in anticipation of working with Patrick.

I had a close friend with a son with Asperger's, so I understood how difficult it could be and I wasn't really sure what I was in for. I wasn't sure how I was going to go about it with him. I got to know that the more fearful and uncomfortable he was, the more childlike behaviors I'd see come out. It took a while for him to realize that I had his best interests at heart.

I didn't treat him any differently from any of my other students. I knew he had to be able to work at a level in this business that would be expected of him, because no one was going to make accommodations for him just because he had a label. I made that clear from the start, and I think he really appreciated that. He doesn't want to be singled out; he wants to fit in. I am directing him like he'll be directed in Hollywood. I'm being super picky and the harder I am on him now, the more he thrives. Voice-over is his happy zone now. The world needs his talent. We're going to make this work!

Cammie's approach unknowingly reflected what the research on hope has shown: Hope is correlated with clear goals that have been set high enough to "stretch" the person. Breaking tasks into small steps sequenced toward larger or long-term goals is also important. High-hope parents and teachers also find multiple pathways to reach goals and try multiple approaches.

Here's a specific example from Cammie's approach with Patrick when he once insisted he "couldn't" do a particular voice.

I wanted Patrick to add new characters to his resume. I had selected some material from the cartoon movie *Kung Fu Panda* and wanted him to work on the character Tai Lung.

When I handed him the copy Patrick immediately said, "I can't do this." He said that he didn't have the right voice, wasn't the right age, and the actor who originally played this role wore shoes that were too big for him to fill. He was adamant that it could NOT be done. He said it was "impossible!"

I reminded Patrick that as a trained voice talent he indeed had the skills to master this task. He wasn't at all convinced, but he was listening to what I said and he didn't cut me off. We discussed the vocal characteristics of this particular character, including the pitch of the voice (deep, resonant, with a bit of gravel), the attitude (cocky and arrogant), and the pacing of his speech (slow and deliberate).

Then I asked Patrick to go up to the microphone and try a few lines. He was still quite skeptical, but he was willing to give it a try.

We recorded a few lines in a few different ways, with support and direction from both his Aunt Mary and me. We both could feel Patrick starting to relax and enjoy himself. But when we listened to his recordings, Pat insisted they still weren't right. Since I hadn't seen the original movie I wasn't exactly sure how to direct him through this, but Mary had a great idea. She said "Let's see if we can find any videos of the movie on YouTube."

Lo and behold, we were able to find a clip of Ian McShane, the actor who voiced Tai Lung in the movie "Kung Fu Panda!" We were mesmerized watching Mr. McShane bring this character to life. After watching the video a couple of times Patrick said, "Okay, I'm ready to try it again."

And so he did. He was able to home in on the subtleties of the complex character and deliver a performance that knocked our socks off! Patrick was beaming behind the mic because he knew that he had nailed the performance. He did it as well as the pro!

Patrick isn't one to pat himself on his own back, but it's obvious that doing voice-over work—and doing it very well—is important to him, and provides deep satisfaction.

Since then, Patrick has used this same technique of watching videos on YouTube to help him develop other characters and dialects, including Russian and Middle Eastern accents.

*Patrick's early special interest has been nurtured
into professional voice-over training.*

Real Life Example #2: Martha Crashes, Redirects, and Rebounds

We asked Martha to tell us more about how she got from college to her clerical job in the Science Department at Sacramento City College. Her story is fascinating. It illustrates numerous important points: how not having a diagnosis can be detrimental, how a person's lack of social skills can override their stellar performance, how a new environment and too much stimulation can be overwhelming, how getting counseling and medication can be critical, and how being flexible while still honoring your interests can eventually lead to a satisfying and meaningful career and life.

> After I graduated from college in 1979, I wasn't sure what to do with myself. I knew I had an interest in foreign cultures, partially because I had an aptitude for foreign languages, and also because I always felt like a misfit in my own culture. I tended to bond more easily with people from foreign countries. (I wasn't diagnosed then, so I had no idea this is typical of people on the spectrum.) So I decided to apply for the Foreign Service exam so I could work as a diplomat in an American embassy overseas. I went through an extensive and selective winnowing process and was hired!

I was unusually young for the typical profile of a Foreign Service officer, since I was only 22, and the average new hire is 35. I was also a very socially immature 22-year-old despite my intelligence. Having no idea I had AS, I was still trying to figure out why I was always out of step and making wrong decisions.

During my first assignment I was stationed in Auckland, New Zealand. I had a supervisor who was much older than I. He was threatened by my intelligence and my ability to finish paperwork much more quickly than he could. In spite of my good technical performance, he rated me very low on my performance evaluation, primarily because my social skills were not that good. In the Foreign Service, if you get anything other than stellar ratings on your performance evaluation, your career is basically over. But I still had over two years guaranteed on my contract, and I hoped I could improve my performance rating.

I was relocated to Warsaw, Poland. By that time I was struggling with depression and anxiety. Then I land in such a foreign environment, and right at the height of the solidarity movement. There were Polish tanks chasing demonstrators down the street in front of our embassy! I was overwhelmed, and I basically had a nervous breakdown. I was medically evacuated back to the States, where I was hospitalized for about three days. I got started on medication for my mood, and while they've had to be adjusted and changed over the years, I remain on them to this day.

They were still obligated to employ me for another two years so I opted to finish out that time, and my remaining assignments were at State Department headquarters in Washington, D.C. When I returned home to Sacramento, all I really had was some clerical skills. I sought work as a temp in various offices and eventually worked my way into medical transcription. This came about because I happened to get a temp assignment at a medical malpractice law office. My job there was to translate dictations of medical charts. I found I really liked that, so when I needed another temp position I asked for something in a medical facility and they assigned me to Sutter Memorial Hospital. I did such a good job for them that they hired me permanently. For the next 15 or so years, I worked at various hospitals and clinics doing medical transcription.

But eventually the industry changed and they started to outsource transcription. I decided to go back to community college for medical coding. I figured an advantage for coding is that social skills are not as important. In fact, even in transcription I worked with many women who were probably on the spectrum, but of course I didn't know it at the time. I did well and completed a two-year program. But I couldn't get hired, despite my good academic record, because I couldn't pass the tests that hospital required.

So then I returned to the idea of clerical work, and applied for openings at our college district and got hired. I think I fit in well here. I work with science professors and there might be some of them on the spectrum, too. When I first started working here I learned about Temple and the spectrum, and I've explained it to a couple of people here. I think the professors appreciate the fact that I am over-qualified, that I do a good job for them, and that I am genuinely interested in science. I have a sense of belonging to a family with these professors that I've never experienced before, and to me that is very valuable.

Martha at her desk in the Science Department

Real Life Example #3: Jaime's Transition from Unmotivated High School Student to Conscientious College Student

Jaime told us he was a "get by" student in high school. He was bright but he barely studied. He thought he was "too smart too study" and says he never even read the full chapters in his high school textbooks. He got B's and that was fine with him.

When he went away to college, he found a very different environment. He says he had to "re-wire" his brain to accept that the only way he was going to be able to succeed in these more challenging courses was to really study. He could no longer just get by. He realized he needed to closely read the material and absorb it, rather than just regurgitating it like he did in high school. He started a habit of reading, then doing practice problems. He realized that he needed to do this consistently.

Jaime chose to major in space physics. As part of this major he had to learn some coding and programming. He learned SQL, HTML, and other languages. These classes were more challenging than high school subjects, and that was a very good thing. His brain engaged in these more technical learning tasks that involved data and numbers. He told us, *"I absolutely love looking at numbers and translating them into something meaningful."*

After graduation, he got a few coding jobs, and then interviewed at one of the giants of the technology world. They liked and appreciated his extensive technical background and his coding skills. He apparently interviewed, though, in a way that came across as different from other candidates.

> I later found out that my supervisor who hired me is married to an Aspie, and she said that she could detect something about my being on the spectrum during the interview. Maybe she could relate to the capacity those of us on the spectrum have.

His interviewer, who unbeknownst to him at the time was to be his supervisor, mentored him and helped him supplement his technical skills with enough additional tools to eventually become a project manager. In this capacity, he handled tasks vital to his company when they were engaged in mergers or acquisitions.

Specifically, he manipulated spreadsheets via Excel with the purpose of detecting any issues the acquired companies had that needed converting to his company's system. He had to be sure that prior to "going live" as part of his company, the new systems had minimal to no errors in their complex, detailed operating systems. This job is well suited to his detail-oriented brain and has earned him substantial positive feedback.

As he has successfully continued at his company, he recently was given the job title of "Business Analyst." Now he works on a team that updates documents in their system via electronic tools, and will soon incorporate business analytics, which he says is something he loves. The more technical his job duties, the more he enjoys them.

PART II

Stretching Your Child
&
Avoiding Pitfalls

CHAPTER 4

Stretching Your Child Just Outside Their Comfort Zone

You can avoid reality, but you cannot avoid the consequences of avoiding reality.

—*Ayn Rand*

Our chief want in life is somebody who will make us do what we can.

—*Ralph Waldo Emerson*

You want your child to develop and mature. You look forward to them learning new skills and coping strategies. But you're torn. Your child or teen on the spectrum often seems to care very little. They seem content to stay right where they are, even if they are miserable. How do you figure out how much and when to push, and when to back off? Nancy, mother of 25-year-old Daniel, found that even the professionals she worked with couldn't agree: *"Half the time they think you're pushing too much, and half the time they think you're not doing enough!"*

In this chapter, we will spell out ways to approach your child so that they have the best odds of moving forward. We'll give you insight into their brain wiring so you can work with that information instead of fighting it. We'll share how several parents found successful pathways forward, even when their children fought them. In the same way we encourage you to lovingly push your child, this chapter is a loving push directed to you.

It can be tough to move our spectrum kids forward, because the autistic brain is usually very sensitive to change and novelty. Routines, rituals, and sameness are the preferred status quo. Even introducing what to you seems to be a minor change can trigger major resistance or meltdowns. Sometimes it just doesn't seem worth the fight. But we're here to tell you that your child depends on you pushing them.

Most of them lack several critical ingredients necessary to push themselves without your active help. First, they struggle to find the initiative to start things outside their special interests. Second, they often have no concept of how important mastering basic skills is to maintaining a household, a job, or financial independence. Third, they frequently battle disorganization, and find it difficult to prioritize and to sustain attention. Difficulty reading social cues, along with a tendency towards isolation, adds to the mix.

While they may defer to others to handle situations, they are seldom willing to actively ask for assistance. They are easily overwhelmed—by frustration, sensory input, and multi-tasking. Finally, if undetected or untreated anxiety or depression is present, this can render even acquired skills unusable.

It's unlikely that your child is lazy in the ordinary sense, even though it might look that way. Actually, they are often doggedly hard workers when immersed in something that they genuinely care about. But a child or teen with autism has a brain that is wired in a way that makes self-initiation difficult most of the time. They are often themselves painfully aware of this challenge.

Your Young Adult Child May *Know* They Need a Push

Daniel, 25, who has a master's degree in math, but is currently unemployed, definitely has insight into his inertia.

> There's stuff I could be doing, but I have a hard time focusing on it. If I get someone to force me to do productive stuff, I do it. I need a program that keeps me on task. Like a program that would do random screen captures and send them to somebody whose opinion I care about. Someone who I wouldn't want seeing that I was wasting time playing Flash games.

Similarly, Patrick's Aunt Mary described how her nephew himself encouraged her to push him.

> I worried sometimes as we got further into his voice lessons that he is so self-critical that he wouldn't keep going. His coach sent him home with homework and at first he was saying, "I can't do this! This is stupid!" My approach is not to just force him but also not to let him throw it all away. We step back and we may not do something the way everybody else might do it, but we will find our own way. He can sit in his room and that will be his reality and he will be afraid to venture out. He knows this is bad and even said to me, "Dr. Moore wants you to push me. You need to push me."

Patrick's father, Ray, says this is still his biggest concern for his son.

> The self-direction is the most difficult part. My goal is for Patrick to be self-reliant and self-supporting. It's hard for him to push himself. I tell him we all have to do things even if they bore us or seem to have no meaning. I tell him we have to do the best we can. Find something you love. If it's not a job, find something else. We try to keep those positive thoughts going, but I'm not all sunshine and rainbows all day. I get aggravated and he has to learn we all do, and we have to get through it. He's good at the aggravation part, but still learning the get-past-it part.

It's About the Specialized Wiring

Pushing is necessary because those on the spectrum are unlikely to automatically pick up the mundane but necessary tasks of daily life without us intentionally nudging then and providing them with information, encouragement, and persistence. Since they often have little curiosity about the world outside their special interests, they seldom come to us and ask us to teach them a skill.

It's not that those on the spectrum don't care what parents or other important people in their lives think. They often care deeply, and they do want to please. But they don't tend to translate that sentiment into self-initiated action.

Autism is characterized by glitches in the brain's executive functioning. The "departments" of the brain don't automatically communicate and come online when presented with a low- or medium-interest task. And without this part of the brain clicking into gear, the ability to plan, organize, and initiate goal-directed behavior is impaired.

Neurotypical children, on the other hand, often find delight and satisfaction in exploring and testing their limits without parental oversight. Their self-confidence grows when they can show off independently learned accomplishments. Their childhoods typically echo with exclamations of "Look at me!" This may not even occur to children on the spectrum.

Daniel's Mom Looks Back

Daniel's mother remembers the wide differences in raising her four sons.

As Daniel was growing up I was trying to teach him and his brothers independence, but it sure didn't happen with him the way it did with our other kids. With Dan, I had to make it intentional and be specific in instructions and expectations. Dan wanted me to make all the decisions. And I have to admit, that I kind of have done that a lot. Like in high school, I'd ask him what he wanted to do, and he'd say "I don't know." So I'd suggest something. And that's kind of how it's gone. He says "Freedom is overrated" and he thinks his world is easier if he doesn't have to make choices.

Looking back, I want to stress to people that you can't just say, "put forth the effort." You have to push them out of complacency. Because how sad for them and what a burden on society if they don't do anything.

Life is More Than Special Interests

The brain of an autistic child will sustain focus if a task falls within their special interest. In this case, the neural connections needed for that specific function go into overdrive. You can think of the autistic brain as analogous to a high-performance car that is capable of going faster and farther than other cars—*when all weather, road, and terrain conditions fit that car perfectly.* But the accelerator pedal requires extra pressure to engage, and the brakes are just the opposite—even slight compression brings everything to a screaming halt. And meeting unexpected obstacles along the way can bring things to an immediate frozen stop.

But life is more than special interests. You must also teach your child or teen general life skills. Without them, your child will not have the foundation for success that is necessary to pursue and maintain their special interests. Even rocket scientists have to get to their job, feed themselves, and pay their bills.

Children on the higher end of the spectrum, though often cognitively ahead (at least in some areas), generally lag behind their peers in emotional and social development. They may also take longer to develop body awareness, and gross and fine motor skills. This combination may mean they learn some tasks more slowly or later than other children. They need extra help to catch up, and jobs or household tasks are a good way to provide them a leg-up.

Jaime, now 35, talked about his gross motor struggles and what has helped. He found that even four months working as a busboy during high school had benefits. Now, as an adult, he's found other useful tips.

> Being a busboy was hard. I spilled water all over people. I'd always struggled with my balance and reflexes. I did get better though as a result of that job, and I still use the techniques I learned when I have to hold multiple things. Now I also go to the gym and have found that's an exceptional way to improve. For example, I've learned when doing an exercise that requires balance that one trick is to focus on a single object visually. That and continuously doing the exercises translates to real life.

A Mind Set to a Default of "NO"

A child with autism has a brain that responds, by default, with "no!" Preferring sameness and routine, autistic children often say "no" before they even think about the question or option they are being presented with. It is their default setting, because as we pointed out before, novelty brings unpredictability, which causes fear. Even familiar activities, if presented as a choice, are often refused, many times even when a child has enjoyed the very same activity in the past. It's not logical; it's a more primitive, emotional part of the brain responding.

Teens and young adults with autism don't necessarily outgrow this, and may even become more stuck in negativity or fear as they become older. As developmental challenges become more daunting, without help, their resistance often rises to match the intensity of the changes entering their lives.

It's vital that parents and professionals expect this response and not be thrown off track by it. Even though it can feel personal, it's not meant to be. Too many parents, teachers, and even therapists get frustrated by endless "no's" and eventually either give in or give up. A smarter approach is to anticipate this default response, work around it when possible, and hit it head-on when necessary.

To create a successful life for children on the spectrum, everyone who cares about them has to be able to stand strong in the face of resistance. Even those in professional roles with children can hold them back if they back down. If your child is involved in a program, make sure everyone there is willing to stick it out when met with resistance. If they periodically cave in the face of your child's "no," they are creating the intermittent reinforcement that greatly escalates your child's determination to avoid challenges and growth.

Barbara's Story of Standing Strong Through Her Tears

Barbara is the mom of a 28-year-old autistic daughter who is verbal but has some intellectual challenges. She now lives successfully in a house with three roommates who share some resources. They spend about five hours a day with a life skills instructor who visits to assist with appointments, and who provides instruction and oversight of household tasks like cooking, shopping, and cleaning. Her mom recalls how painful it was to stick to a decision she knew would ultimately help her daughter.

Cara was just getting ready to graduate from a program that was designed to prepare her for greater independence. The plan all along had been that she would move out of my home into a structured living situation with peers. They were preparing her to be able to successfully take care of her basic daily activities and to make a contribution vocationally. We had worked very hard to find a place for her to move into.

So just before graduation, I'm in Nordstrom's one day and she calls me crying hysterically. "I want to come home! I'm scared and I want to live with you for the rest of my life!" I started crying on the phone too, but managed to tell her, "Cara, you worked very hard to learn how to be independent and you can't live with me the rest of your life because one day I am going to die, like all living things. It's not a good plan. You want to learn to live a happy life."

I remember this conversation well (the salespeople in Nordstrom's probably do too, since I was wandering around in a daze while I was crying and talking on the phone, and I know they were all looking at me). I felt horrible, like I was abandoning her. But the logical part of me knew I wanted her to be independent. All of us parents ARE going to die, and we have to get our kids to live their lives as though we're not going to be there. Because the fact is, we're not. And by letting them learn everything possible they can do for themselves, that's one less thing they don't need you for when you're not around.

But boy, did I feel like shit. I was telling her she couldn't come home. I wasn't being selfish, but it sure felt that way.

I think to create successful lives for our kids, we have to step back even further than parents of NT kids. We have to give our kids the opportunity to succeed and the opportunity to fail. Because only by doing those two things can they move forward. The success teaches them they can do things. The failure teaches them they have to try again.

The Need for Customized Approaches

Adults may assume a child can't learn, when in fact that child just needs a different approach. Neurotypical children can often learn via multiple sensory channels, sometimes all at once. They learn by listening, reading, observing, taking in emotions, and registering sensory input. That type of flexible, multi-channeled learning doesn't happen as often with children on the spectrum, whose brain wiring tends to be specialized. While still holding our children accountable, it sometimes helps to modify their projects or chores if necessary so they can learn easier. Otherwise, they may get further and further behind their peers as the years pass. Suddenly, they're teens and have not acquired the basic skills necessary to navigate the world.

The outside push we provide to spectrum children cannot be presented ambiguously or in general terms. They have to be plainly and obviously told that others expect them to contribute. At home, parents have to make it clear that each member is assigned household tasks. These expectations should be concrete, and duties must be broken into clear step-by-step directions. Each undertaking should be first modeled, and then observed, before expecting your child to do it. Creating a set time for each task to be done builds routines, which then become habits.

Daniel's Recommendations for Parents

Daniel, who commented above about his problems with focusing, had this to say when asked how he would recommend parents help their children on the spectrum learn new things.

> I think I'd try to push them. I'd push them to do something productive and then make them show it off to me. Mostly I'd leave it to them to choose tasks, but it would have to be something tangible. I know I need people to push me to try things. Then I will do it. I get used to things quickly. The first two times might be hard, but then it's easy and normal, and I have no trouble doing it all the time. It becomes a routine.

Most children and teens on the spectrum share Daniel's affinity for routine. Once a task is broken into clear steps and those steps are repeated, they are seldom forgotten. They also tend to be adhered to thoroughly and without deviation. The down side of this is that it allows for little flexibility or generalizing. These aspects must be thought of ahead of time when teaching skills.

For example, let's say you want to teach your teen how to do laundry. They obviously need to learn how to operate the washer and dryer, but they need a different type of instruction than NT teens. They will not necessarily try to figure out all the settings or ask questions. They will not automatically know how to tell if something needs washing to begin with. It will probably take longer for you to teach your autistic teen, but simply put, it's critical. The consequences to you of not teaching basic tasks will consume even more time and effort later. If no one shows them how (over and over!) they won't necessarily just "pick it up" no matter how high their IQ is.

Autistic individuals also frequently appear to live "in the moment" and fail to think ahead and anticipate the long-term consequences of their behavior. They rarely self-reflect or monitor themselves. They're also frequently impulsive, and often struggle to appropriately delay gratification or inhibit inappropriate responses.

Stick to the Basics Instead of Making It Complicated

Sometimes our neurotypical minds make things more difficult! When you are teaching a child on the spectrum(or anyone, really) a new task, keep it simple. Find the basic principle and emphasize it directly and repeatedly. Don't get sidetracked with unimportant or minor details. Before you attempt to teach something, figure out what your priority is. Teach that principle and forget the rest.

Temple has found that many times her work in livestock facilities comes down to simple changes. The company may think they have a complicated problem, but the fix may actually be straightforward and simple. A machine needs a basic repair. The surface of the floor needs to be changed to non-slip. These are not complicated changes. Temple has learned to pay very close attention to details, so she can find the main principle at work and go from there.

Even when addressing more complex issues, such as animal welfare, Temple breaks it down into "critical control points." What is really going to make a difference in the end? There could be hundreds of variables, but which ones are critical to outcome? In her work, she's identified just five measures that, if controlled, distinguish safe, efficient livestock facilities from the ones that ignore these factors. Lots of other details can also be manipulated, but they really don't make much difference. Critical control theory works on the principle that you can find a few vital things to measure, and those few things will tell you everything important you need to know. A relatively few variables can assess a multitude of problems.

Critical control points also exist for children on the spectrum. Their ability to take turns, to cope with not always getting their way, to be willing to do some things they really don't want to do, to control impulsive behavior, to maintain basic hygiene, and to be able to follow through on tasks (household chores as a young child, volunteer work or helping others as a teen, and work assignments as an adult) influence a myriad of downstream behaviors. If we assess these areas when kids are young, make sure our children gain ability in these critical areas, and continually monitor their behavior on these tasks, we automatically eliminate many other problems.

Keep this in mind as you lovingly push your child. Assess the critical control points—what areas need work? Then figure out the most important steps of that task, and stick to them. Be specific, and don't be long-winded when you tell your child what you expect of them. If you can't explain it simply, you probably need to rethink it.

Avoiding Perfectionism

Kids on the spectrum often get stuck because they strive for perfection. When they don't achieve it, they get frustrated and want to give up. They also don't want to try things if they aren't sure they can do it perfectly. When Temple encounters this, she explains to people that even highly skilled professionals make mistakes, because no one achieves constant perfection. She uses the example of *National Geographic* photographers—arguably the best in the business. If you look closely enough, though, you can find technical errors even in *National Geographic*.

Your child may be intolerant not only of their own mistakes, but also of those of others, including yours. Be sure you aren't a perfectionist yourself, because your kid will sense it and your actions will speak louder than words. When you make a mistake and your kid sees it, acknowledge it and tell them what you've learned from it.

In other words, teach your child that mistakes are simply data that they then use to adjust the next step. Give them examples of mistakes made that resulted in successes. For example, the development of penicillin resulted from Sir Alexander Fleming, a scientist, throwing away his Petri dishes after he "failed" to discover the drug he was searching for. Only then did he discover a mold that was dissolving all the bacteria around it. You can find other examples easily by doing an Internet search for "mistakes that turned into successes." This would be a good activity to do with your child.

Sarah, who relies on her husband for helpful feedback and support, said that she could really relate to the struggle with perfectionism.

My husband helped me see what a perfectionist I have always been and how hard I am on myself. He said I didn't have to be perfect, so my decisions didn't have to be perfect. I used to take forever to decide anything. But he explained to me that I could always decide something and then later change my mind. This was a new concept for me!

Before then I simply wouldn't decide things, and instead I would be constantly anxious as a result. I used to edit myself all the time. I was so bad that I wouldn't even finish sentences. But he helped me see that however something I'm saying comes out, it's all right. It doesn't have to be perfect. That has helped me speak much more freely and try more new things.

Sarah also had another example of a lesson she learned about counting on perfection from others—in this case expecting it from a dog. By seeing herself through the eyes of a dog trainer, she realized that this was sabotaging both her and the dog!

My husband and I decided to get a dog, and I immediately began looking online for information on dogs, breeds, training, etc. We decided to get a yellow lab, but after many introductions to various dogs that didn't seem to fit, we found a young female golden retriever. She was very good tempered and patient, and seemed to behave as if she was grateful for being rescued.

Since I had been watching many videos on dog training, I was certain that I could teach the dog a few things about obedience, including walking on a leash, and the standard sit, stay, come, wait, and other basic commands. But I quickly felt frustrated that the dog didn't seem to understand what I wanted, and it seemed to continue behaviors that I considered non-compliant. My husband joined me one day as I walked the dog, to see if he could offer some insight. He immediately mentioned to me that I was being impatient and inconsistent with my commands, and had expectations that exceeded the dog's ability. I continued to work with the dog for many months and continued to feel frustrated that the dog wasn't doing the commands right. My husband continued to remind me that I needed to be patient and consistent, which I believed I was, yet the dog continued to seem to do what it wanted. Despite increasing the time I spent working with the dog, the training I was offering the dog seemed to work only sometimes.

In time, I found two professional dog trainers. The first one was helpful, but the problems seemed to come back intermittently, despite the number of hours a day that I worked. Since I remained frustrated, I took a break from working with the dog and later found a new trainer that had experience working with service dogs for ASD. She watched me work with the dog and noted that I was impatient, inconsistent with the words I used for commands, and used body language that the dog thought meant one thing when I thought it meant another.

Luckily, dogs forgive very quickly. The new trainer taught me to use very basic and simple commands, request very clear and reasonable actions from my dog, and provide immediate positive or negative reinforcement. The difference was amazing for both me and my dog, who now seemed to understand almost everything I wanted. She behaved great nearly every time it was expected of her. I found myself surprised at how fast she learned.

I was expecting my dog to listen the first time, learn the command within just a couple of times of trying it, and remember it every time, perfectly. Wanting her to be immediately perfect only caused me a great deal of stress, and caused the dog confusion and discomfort. I am the one that had something to learn from the trainer: I had to learn to read my dog's body language and let her have time to learn mine. When that happened, and when I learned to be patient and objectively responsive, and accept that she will try hard but not be perfect, my dog worked even harder to do what I wanted, and I didn't have to work so hard.

It was a very difficult and time-consuming lesson, to learn that expecting perfection only resulted in stress and frustration, and kept me from achieving my goal of having a well-behaved (not perfect, but good enough), loving, and pleasing dog. I continue to remind myself every day of this lesson.

Sarah and her service dog Ginger, who both learned important lessons.

Finding the Best Pace for Your Child

Pace is important when your child needs a loving push. You need to know your child's rhythms so that you can plan ahead. The worst time to try to push your child out of their comfort zone is when they are already annoyed or distressed. Find a time they are rested, not hungry, and not overwhelmed by sensory input.

Start small, and even then know you're likely to get pushback. That's part of the deal, and it's your job to combine acknowledgement of the discomfort with continuing to move forward. If you back off, your child learns that expressing distress is the ticket to getting you to stop pushing and let them return to their comfort zone.

You might think that backing off once in awhile won't hurt anything, but consider this: The most powerful type of reinforcement is intermittent. If our actions sometimes produce our desired result (but not always), we're primed to work even harder because we know that with enough attempts we'll be rewarded. This reinforcement pattern actually mimics addiction. Las Vegas casino owners know this well, and have made a science of knowing just how many times their slot machines need to pay out in order to hook the most customers! Don't hook your child by intermittently giving them the reward of backing off when they start to show resistance.

An Example of Starting Small

Here's an example of starting small. Debra thinks Patrick wanted to believe others when they told him he was funny, had a good singing voice, and was a great mimic. But his confidence hadn't developed enough to trump his fear of failure. It would have been too much too soon to simply tell him he could use these talents in a job.

His Aunt Mary started very small. She had him listen to an opera recording. One day she had him sing a line from "West Side Story" while they were in the car. It was a tough, high note to hit ("Maria!"), and Patrick nailed it. With Patrick's permission, Mary emailed Debra about the incident so we could piggyback on that step in therapy. When I asked Patrick about it, he gave an encore performance, which was delightful and genuinely impressive. Another small step in building confidence. Mary then researched voice teachers. She found a singing coach and took an unenthusiastic Patrick to meet him. The teacher had him sing scales, and while he did well (and had never done it before), Patrick's reaction to the idea of singing was a less than lukewarm "It's okay."

In the meantime, we had been brainstorming other options for getting Patrick out into the world in a way that might be enjoyable and would give him the opportunity to "check out," without pressure, other similar creative activities. It turned out there was a small, informal improvisational class offered nearby through the parks and recreation district. Patrick wasn't ready to go alone, but his father and his younger brother said they'd go and participate too. Another step. While Patrick decided he wasn't interested in joining an improv group, he realized that everyone seemed to accept him and he felt supported and even had some fun.

Patrick's aunt knew she had to move at his pace, saying, "I knew I needed to SLOWLY introduce ideas and experiences, but I wasn't going to let go of it." She let a few weeks go by after the singing coach, and then took Patrick to a voice-over coach. Patrick's aunt is wise and knows her nephew well. She also understands the autistic brain, from personal experience of growing up with Patrick's mom, who has also been diagnosed on the spectrum. She makes a very important point: "To get autistic kids to progress, they must DO things, not just talk about them."

She added, "Even small successes may be taxing for Patrick. He needs more than the average success before he will own it, and even then his negative voice is so loud. You have to keep at it, and keep trying things, because you never know when you'll hit on something that will keep him motivated. Even then you have to keep him actively involved with it or his brain will knock it down. It took a year of voice-over lessons before we could see and feel his proud energy. It was worth it!"

Deadlines and Consequences are Part of Pacing

Give your child deadlines when you assign them a task. They need to know when they have to start the task and when it has to be finished. Can you imagine a teacher letting your child turn in homework "whenever you feel like it" or not assigning a specific day that a paper has to be finished? What about an employer—can you imagine them telling your teen to do an assignment at their leisure and if they never do complete it, that's acceptable? In the first example, your child would get a failing grade, and in the second they would be fired. That's real life. Do your child a favor and prepare them for it now.

You need to tell your child what will happen if a task is not started or finished on time. The negative consequences have to really mean something to your child. So for example, let's say you decide it's high time for your teen to clean their room. You tell them exactly what that means. You don't just say, "Clean your room." To them that might mean picking up one piece of clothing off the floor! You make a list, you review it with them and show them how to do each step, and you observe them doing each step the first time to be sure they understand. You make sure they can envision what the outcome of successful task completion looks like. For instance, picking up clothes from the floor and moving them to a chair is not a successful outcome; hanging them in the closet is. You give them a specific day and time you will inspect their work. You give them the consequence of not cleaning their room in advance before they start the task.

For example, "If you leave any of these steps undone, you will have to stop whatever you are doing when I check on the job at 5:00 like we agreed, and do them right away. It doesn't matter what you are in the middle of, you will have to stop it. If you do not immediately stop, in addition to still having to do the task, you will be restricted from computer time until it is satisfactorily completed."

If that sounds harsh to you, remind yourself how the real adult world works. And remember that your child depends on you to prepare them for it.

Don't Let Guilt Undermine You

Some parents have built up a storehouse of guilt over the years. Watching your child struggle—socially, academically, and emotionally—is a heartbreaking experience. Undoubtedly you've lost your cool at times, or been too tired to intervene or stick to a plan. It's normal to have questions about choices you've made along the way. But don't let those feelings turn into guilt that handicaps your child. You can't make up for the past by backing off now. Preparing your child for the next phase of life has to be your unwavering focus.

It's a normal human tendency for parents to be highly protective of a child on the spectrum, knowing their social and emotional vulnerabilities. It's understandable that you may feel you are the only one to "get" and "protect" your child.

We caution you, though, not to do things for your child that they might be able to master themselves. Viewing and interacting with your child mainly from a protective stance can lead them to getting stuck below their capabilities. You may have prematurely accepted that your child can't make progress in a particular area, when this isn't the case at all. It's bad enough that others will sometimes underestimate your child. Don't be one of them.

Talk Bluntly to Your Child About Responsibility

Children, teens, and even many young adults don't usually think in terms of responsibility to others unless it has been woven into their upbringing. If you believe your child hasn't internalized this value, it's time to have a blunt conversation with them about it. Tell them it is their responsibility to be their best and to contribute to their family, to others, and to the world. Have an idea of what appropriate contributions are for various ages.

Assuming your child is not severely cognitively impaired, a young child is capable of brushing their teeth, putting toys away, and greeting others appropriately. Elementary school children are capable of doing homework, making their bed, helping set and clear the table, and tidying up personal belongings. By middle school, kids can help with many household chores, such as folding laundry, making their own sandwiches, and loading the dishwasher. They should also help out others, including people outside the immediate family. This is a foundation that will help them socially and vocationally. Being helpful gives them practice with social skills, and other practical life skills like showing up when they say they're going to. Examples could be setting up chairs for a church event, taking food to an ill neighbor, or helping with a community garage sale. Being responsible for a pet or a small garden is also good preparation for later responsibilities.

By high school most teens on the higher end of the autism spectrum should be doing laundry, starting to practice driving, managing money, opening a savings account, and able to shop independently. By now you want them to be involved with a volunteer or paying job, even if it is very part time.

We're not giving kids with autism a break if we neglect to hold them accountable for these sorts of tasks. Instead, we are setting them up to be unprepared when they are suddenly out of high school and faced with the real world.

Hold Them Responsible While Still Recognizing Their Unique Needs

Kids on the spectrum can often do more than we think, as long as we appreciate their unique ways of processing information. Autistic kids may need to go more slowly, to have tasks broken down into smaller steps, and to have more repetition before something "sticks." Auditory thinkers may do fine with verbal instructions, but visual learners need to have detailed, written information and visual reminders. Almost all spectrum kids need direct, hands-on experience in order to integrate information. Show them one step of a task, have them ask any questions, show them again, then have them show you. Repeat until they can do it without mistakes. Take a break if needed. Then add the next step, and repeat. As Ray, Patrick's father, said, "If you have a child with Asperger's, get ready to repeat yourself. Because you will—constantly!"

Patrick's mom gave these examples of what happened when she tried to teach him two different household chores. They illustrate the need to work with your kid to figure out the best way for them to accomplish a task. Pat didn't get off the hook—he learned both tasks—but his mom was really smart in how she approached him.

I decided to teach Pat to sweep the kitchen floor. Even though he huffed about it, he didn't run away. Cool. So, I started to sweep and explain what I was doing. You have to sweep in a certain pattern so you know you've covered everywhere. Just follow the tile. And he says, "Why are you sweeping there? I don't see anything." Well, just cuz you can't see it … "Can't I just sweep where I can see the dirt? This doesn't make sense." If you just follow the pattern, you'll be surprised how much dirt is really here. Just try. I gave him the broom, and he started to sweep rather awkwardly. I stared at him hard …what's different? He's holding the broom with the opposite hand-grip, sweeping in the opposite direction. I felt that was weird because we're both right-handed. "This doesn't feel right. I can't do this! Here —you do it. I'm no good at this physical stuff!"

"Wait, wait, try it this way," and I showed him the classic way to hold the handle and asked him to sweep in the opposite direction. You know, he was actually more awkward than before. Frustrated, he angrily gave me back the broom and continued voicing his negative thoughts down the hallway to his room, and slammed and locked his bedroom door.

Wait. What just happened? As I meditated for a while, I realized … he really is wired differently. I picked up the broom, switched my hand positions, and tried sweeping his way; a bit awkward but do-able. Yelling through his door … "Pat, Pat! I tried it the way you do it and it works just fine!" It just never occurred to me to switch hands. I had to be willing to think about it and try it his way.

The same thing happened with making scrambled eggs. For the longest time he wouldn't make them: "I can't do this." I could never figure out why he was stuck on this. But then he wanted to learn to make an omelet and while I was showing him, I got to see what the problem was. He was scrambling his eggs counter-clockwise—which I tried. It's not easy to do! He'd scramble for a while and then hand over the spatula to me to finish it up. I thought "Well, at least he's asking for help." In this case I found a gadget that smoothly whisks the eggs with a turning knob. It works great. "See, Pat? I found a way that works for you." He makes a great omelet now!

Patrick preparing breakfast for the family.

When It's Time to Kick It Up a Notch—Do It! A Father's Example

The optimal pace for learning is one that keeps your child moving forward without being too overwhelmed. Stretching and learning new things usually involves at least mild discomfort, but it shouldn't be severe or incapacitating. If your child is perfectly comfortable, though, it's not likely they are growing. In that case, it's time to kick it up a notch.

You want your child's brain to be in a zone of positive arousal – paying attention, interested, and challenged. Being totally relaxed is actually not what you want. Notice their reactions and adjust accordingly. If they become overwhelmed, help out while continuing to require they do their part.

A beautiful example of this came from John, Daniel's father. It's a great illustration of helping, but also letting your child do as much as they can, even when it's hard.

> I was the Boy Scout master for our local troop. When my son was about 16, we did a 50-mile backpacking trip as one of the activities. That was a push for him. Well, it turned out that the trail was steeper than I expected, and he had a hard time keeping up. I happened to have a hiking stick with me, so when I thought he really wasn't going to make it, I threaded his backpack through the stick and put one end

of it on his shoulder and the other end on mine. We both put out effort and he made it!

Start Early and Build Up Skills That Will Endure

Our society's social norms and parenting styles have become much more informal over the past 50 years. You may or may not agree that this is a good thing. It could be argued, though, that for autistic children, this loosening of standards makes it more challenging to learn self-regulation and social skills. The old-fashioned "rules" may make it easier for autistic children to function, because it's calming for them to have explicit and predictable expectations.

When Temple grew up in the 1950s, social roles and expectations were made clear to kids as soon as they could talk. Children were expected to interact with adults in prescribed ways. They certainly didn't address them by first name; they used titles like "Mr., Miss, or Mrs." or "sir or ma'am." They were admonished if they didn't routinely use certain social niceties such as "please," "thank you," and "you're welcome." But these days, parents are more likely to overlook or dismiss these courtesies.

Temple's mother (and others in her community) made it clear that she could and would use these social graces. It prepared her for later successful interactions and gave her a script so that she knew how to start and end social interactions. It was good, early practice for later learning more advanced skills.

Everything Your Child Does is Life Preparation—Examples from Marina's Mom

Loretta, whose now 33-year-old daughter Marina who was profiled in Chapter 1, spoke about how she approached helping her daughter learn and grow.

> I was always preparing Marina for eventual adulthood—I think consciously by the time she was two years old! I believed everything she did would eventually turn into life skills. Some of the things I tried

she took to—others not so much! I had her care for animals, help her sisters clean up and cook a meal, and wash and sort the clothes. I had her fix her sisters' hair. That she wasn't so hot about! We played lots of games, and she had to read the rules, follow the instructions, and not cheat.

I thought, "I have to find a way for her to survive." I decided I had to keep it simple. I had to do little things to simplify her life so that she could always remember and learn. For example, I bought the same clothes for her and her sisters, just in different colors. I knew she wanted to copy her sisters, who dressed neatly, and sure enough she copied them exactly.

She liked stories, so when I had a chore for her, I made a story out of it. If I wanted her to feed her dog, I'd say that the "princess" wants a piece of cake but can't have it until she feeds her doggie—otherwise she would not be a good person. Marina would envision herself as the good princess—she had good morals—and she was determined to accomplish things. I had to channel her determination. Once she did the chore I often rewarded her with an apple or a cherry, or playing a game together. But I also taught her that she couldn't always expect a reward, and that no one owed her anything. I told her I would always thank her, though.

Marina remembers those days and believes that her mother's approach helped.

As a child I was taught to obey and follow rules. This has helped me throughout my life to have a degree of self-control. I also learned basic skills like creating shopping lists and using calculators. Now I can take inventory of what things we need for the house, make a list, and then go shopping. I learned to cook when I was six, shortly after I learned to read. My mom had tons of cookbooks and we were often left at home with our older sister, so we did a lot of cooking and baking to pass the time. I learned these skills from my mom.

It Takes a Village—The Story of a Neighbor's Impact

Like most kids, those on the spectrum often find it easier to learn from someone other than a parent! Sarah, the wildlife biologist who is indebted to her teachers, also gives substantial credit to her neighbor Armida as someone who facilitated her growth. Armida described how she approached expanding Sarah's skills.

Sarah and her mom and brother were our neighbors from the time she was about 10. My husband and I ran a restaurant that was just down the street and we had to work long hours, often not getting home until 10:00 or 10:30 at night. I thought Sarah would be a perfect babysitter as long as I took it slow and taught her the skills she'd need. At first Sarah didn't know how to cook for the kids or how to change diapers or even how to clean up after herself and them. She didn't have a sense of appropriate routines for the kids or how to entertain them.

I'm not sure what we started with—probably the basics of changing diapers! I had to teach her basics—how to be aware of when the kid peed. So she had to develop an awareness of whether the baby was comfortable or uncomfortable. She had to use her own judgment to figure it out, since the baby obviously couldn't tell her. This was daunting to her at first. But we broke it down and she learned to do it just fine.

I also needed to teach her how to think about what the kids needed. We talked about it together so she'd start to think for herself instead of me just telling her. What time is reasonable for the kids to go to bed, Sarah? What do they need to do before they go to bed? What makes sense in terms of the order of these things? She learned to make a routine for baths, brushing teeth, and getting to bed. At first she didn't want to give them their baths, so we broke that down too.

Then she had to figure out what to do with the kids while they were awake. I didn't want them just watching TV. So we talked about art projects and crafts and reading to the boys. And the kids needed to eat! At first I would leave prepared food for them, but I also was teaching her to cook, so eventually she was able to do this herself.

Even after she went away to college, Sarah would call Armida every couple of weeks and ask how to cook something she'd bought at the market.

A Sister and the Lessons She Learned

Maria, whose brother is Jaime, the 35-year-old technology company employee, spoke about the experience of having both a brother on the spectrum and now a 4½-year-old daughter who was diagnosed a year ago.

Now we know much more about autism. With Jaime, who is on the higher end of the spectrum, we didn't realize so much. We just thought he was a quiet kid who didn't have a lot of friends and kept to himself. We knew he was very intelligent, but he didn't have friends like my older brother and I did. With my daughter being diagnosed early, I can start now to teach her things. I definitely think she needs to learn to express herself. She gets frustrated if she doesn't understand or can't find her words. I try to calm her down with breathing before she has a meltdown, and I talk her through it instead of just getting frustrated. At the same time, I don't baby her or she will never reach the point she needs to reach. Sometimes she just has to go through the emotions and then we talk about it when she's calm.

She dresses herself, puts her dirty clothes in the hamper, puts her dirty dishes in the sink, picks up her toys, and says "please" and "thank you." Her cognitive skills are fantastic. She knows all her shapes already—like hexagons and octagons. But smarts aren't the only skill she'll need. She can be smart all she wants, but you also have to have kindness and you have to share. Teaching them compassion and kindness is a huge part of being able to live in society as an adult on the spectrum.

She adds that as an adult Jaime calls her every day—just to check in and talk. She asks herself, "Who is this person?" and says it wasn't like that when he was younger.

It's bizarre. I'm the emotional one—the huggy, kissy one. Now Jaime is like that! I'm happy for him. He's found himself and is comfortable with who he is now.

CHAPTER 5

What to Do When Your Kid Doesn't Seem to Care or Is Chronically Anxious

Don't let your mind bully your body into believing

it must carry the burden of its worries.

—*Astrid Alauda*

It's a sign of strength to put your hand out and ask for help,

whether it's a friend or a professional or whatever.

—*Bruce Springsteen*

Anxiety and depression commonly co-exist with autism and Asperger's syndrome. Sensory overwhelm, which is pervasive for some on the spectrum, can be one cause of horrible anxiety and panic responses. Even mild chronic anxiety is very discouraging and can result in secondary depression. Mood problems must be tackled, because they can stop your child from moving forward in life. Mood shapes your child's sense of self, their social behaviors, and their ability to follow through with educational and vocational goals. When depression or anxiety is present and untreated, struggles related to autism are worse. By dealing with these issues, your child will have an easier time creating a successful adult life.

Stephanie, mom of 18-year-old Cosette, points out that sometimes it is difficult to recognize how much anxiety a child is enduring.

We really couldn't see or appreciate the extent of her anxiety until we were able to control and get a better handle on some of her autism symptoms. After she matured some, and we were able to get her emotional IQ up near her intellectual IQ, we could then deal with her fears. She worked with her therapist to recognize and alleviate her anxiety triggers, and she's been given some relaxation techniques that have been helpful. She has also gained a lot of relief through medication. I didn't medicate her as a child. But as a teen, she has been on two different medications and these have made a world of difference for her.

Depression is also common, and some studies estimate almost 40% of spectrum children will experience at least one significant episode. While your child is unlikely to volunteer this information, suicidal thoughts are common in Asperger's syndrome, especially during the teen and young adult years.

In addition to genetic vulnerability, other factors increase the odds that a child or teen will become depressed. The brighter and more insightful your child is, the more they recognize their challenges. These kids perceive themselves the most critically, which correlates with worse depression. This holds true for young adults as well.

Anxiety and depression can both get worse when the hormonal changes of puberty hit. Your child's brain and body are both changing; they have no control over this process, and they usually hate it.

In addition to these biological changes, your child's environment during this period can add stress. Junior and senior high school bring more social and sensory challenges. Neurotypical kids suddenly have new interests, including flirting, dating, and fashion. They often leave childhood interests behind. NT boys, in particular, start jockeying for alpha status among their peers, and increased bullying can be part of this dance. Your child can be the target.

Classes are larger, and hallways and cafeterias are more crowded and noisier. Academic demands also shift. Classes require more original writing, your child is expected to think more abstractly, and they have to juggle a greater number of assignments and projects. Some kids react to these changes by retreating, and others by acting out. In either case, they may be miserable.

Temple's Experience Is Typical of Many Autistic People

At the age of 14, Temple hit puberty and her nervous system went into miserable overdrive. She was constantly frightened or had terrible headaches or stomach upset. She had no idea what was causing the anxiety, since it grabbed her unpredictably.

After trying for 20 years to figure out psychological reasons for her anxiety and panic, she came to realize that her nervous system was out of whack and on constant alert. By age 30 she realized her health was now in serious jeopardy, and that she also risked becoming housebound out of fear of panic attacks.

At this point, she set out to find an explanation for her symptoms. She went to every doctor in town and even had a brain scan but no one had answers. Then at age 34 she had to have surgery to remove a skin cancer from her eyelid. That threw her system over the edge and her panic attacks struck even more forcefully. At this near-breaking point she turned to the psychiatric literature and found a journal article that described symptoms just like hers. It said there were antidepressant medications that could control them.

But she didn't like the idea of taking drugs and even though she was miserable, it took a while for her to ask her doctor to try a low dose of an antidepressant. Within two days of taking Tofranil (imipramine) in 1980, she felt 90% better! She was able to stop behaviors that she had been stuck in. For example, before medication she sequestered herself in her room and buried herself in reading in order to calm down. Plus she had been typing compulsively to get her thoughts down on paper. These mad typing sprees stopped after going on medication.

Over the course of the next years, other more subtle changes ensued. Her posture straightened, her talks became smoother and better, her speech became more relaxed, and her eye contact improved. She continues to take a low dose of medication, switching to Norpramin (desipramine) in 1983. To this day, she regards herself as one of the people in the autism community who was saved by medication. She plans to continue taking it.

Your Child Has Probably Been Bullied (But May Not Tell You)

Bullying is highly predictive of depression and anxiety. Researchers at Oxford University who studied 4,000 teens found that the ones who said they were frequent victims of bullying were three times as likely to be depressed at age 18 as their non-bullied peers. One researcher who polled parents found that seventy-seven percent of them reported that their spectrum child had been bullied at school within the last month.

Scott, now in his late 20s, described his earlier struggles.

> I became severely anxious as a teen. I worried horribly about my social peers and how they would react to even the most innocuous-seeming things I did. I was being fairly mercilessly singled out by some rather aggressive bully-types at school. My symptoms only really abated when the bullies dropped out in junior year.

You Must Reduce Sensory Overload

If your child is anxious, always evaluate their environment for sensory overload, especially at school. Don't expect teachers to recognize how this causes your child distress. You need to get in the classroom and see for yourself. Then you need to figure out what has to change to help your child learn. If that means wearing earplugs to muffle noise, or a visor in a classroom full of fluorescent lights, put your advocacy hat on and get a meeting scheduled with school personnel.

At the same time, don't do all the work for your child. Empower them by having them join you in the meeting, and have them prepare a script ahead of time so they can voice the problem themselves. You won't be there in college or in their workplace to advocate for them. They need to practice now, when you're there to shape their requests toward win-win outcomes.

Creatively Reducing Sensory Overload: Cosette's "Poppleton" Glasses

Cosette talks about her anxiety, its relationship to sensory issues, and how her Mom found creative ways to help her.

> Most often, my anxiety was linked to overwhelming situations, new things, sensory overload, strange people, or crowds. Since anxiety of-

ten led to temper tantrums, my parents put me on medication. The first effective drug was Risperidone (Risperdal), which I took regularly for several years. Later, when I started having severe panic attacks, I tried Celexa (which caused side effects in me) and then Prozac, which was extremely effective.

Another thing that helped was a creative adaptation my Mom made for me to help with sensory overload. When I was very young, I was terribly sensitive to noise, bright lights, and to having too many things in my visual field. My Mom made me what she called "Poppleton glasses," after a character in a book I read as a child.

The Poppleton series by Cynthia Rylant was about a talking pig that went on adventures with his friends. In one story, Poppleton became overwhelmed while stargazing, so his friend made him a blindfold with tiny holes cut into it so he could stargaze without seeing every single star. My Mom adapted this into a pair of polarized sunglasses, which she colored all over with a Sharpie marker except for two tiny slots that I used to look out. This helped with the bright lights and the large amounts of merchandise and shelves around stores. They allowed only a tolerable bit of the world in at a time.

Also, for years, I would bring construction headphones with me whenever I went to the movies. Theaters like to turn up the sound very, very loud so the entire room can hear the movie, which was unpleasant for me. I wore them at every film I attended, until one day I forgot them and realized I didn't need them anymore.

I also had severe problems with scratchy textures of clothes, especially tags. My parents carefully cut the tags out of every single item of clothing I wore, and for several years the only pants that I would wear were soft, loose cloth pants called "gauchos." It would be years before I would even dare touch a pair of jeans, and even then only the softest and loosest pairs.

Why OCD (Obsessive Compulsive Disorder) Should Be Considered

The routines and rituals that are often part of autism can be difficult to distinguish from obsessive-compulsive disorder (OCD), a particular type of anxiety disorder. If a child's rituals are excessive and accompanied by anxiety, get someone who knows both OCD and autism to do an evaluation that includes direct observation as well as psychological testing. There are effective therapies and medications that may greatly help your child. Debra received many referrals from a wise colleague who directed an OCD treatment program. People would come to her clinic with a diagnosis of OCD and she'd realize they probably also (or entirely) had undiagnosed autism. Even otherwise good therapists, if unfamiliar with autism, can mistake the social fears and unusual rituals of someone on the spectrum for OCD or miss the autism part.

A clear diagnosis is important, because a person with autism needs a different kind of treatment for obsessions or compulsions. Standard exposure therapy may make things worse. Medications, and their dosages, may also need to be different.

Your Teen Will Likely Need a Loving Push to Get Help

Your teen or adult child is unlikely to ask you for help with their emotional struggles. Once again, they'll need a loving push from you. There are many things you can do that will make a difference, and this chapter will walk you through them.

You should ask your child if they're depressed or anxious, but don't expect them to necessarily admit it. Some don't even recognize their internal state, and some fear being labeled or treated. This seems especially true for depression, and may sadly reflect the tolerance they've developed to a chronic condition. It's like expecting a goldfish to be aware they are wet. For some kids, it's just the way it's always been.

Others may be afraid to acknowledge depression or anxiety for fear of your judgment. In some families, acknowledging the need for outside help is equivalent to admission of failure, evoking shame and embarrassment. This seems especially true of fathers, and they need to be told in no uncertain terms that depriving their child of potential help is unfair and neglectful.

Begin With the Basics—You Can't Skip This Part!

Begin by taking a hard look at the basics of your child's daily routine. You need to eliminate bad habits that reinforce learned helplessness. These habits make mood problems worse. They have to be replaced with experiences that foster confidence and mastery. Here's an example. Let's say you get into daily battles with your child about putting away and hanging up their clothes at the end of the day. You make repeated requests and your teen ignores you. Eventually you yell at them. That works half the time, but you and they both end up frustrated. Too often you give up and do the job yourself. You have now taught your child that if they ignore you long enough they get out of doing the chore.

This pattern has to be broken. A better approach is to designate clearly marked places for various clothes items, and walk your child through a successful completion of the task during a time they're not upset. Later, after they do the task successfully, give them immediate feedback and thanks. If they argue with you, ignore them and do not finish the task yourself. If they do not complete the task, remove a privilege.

Your child may be more upset in the short term, but remember the section on learned helplessness in chapter two. Learned helplessness is directly tied to depression. All the medicine and therapy in the world can't stand up to ongoing bad habits and helplessness.

The Links Between Autism and Mood Problems

Autism, depression, and anxiety share many features. They all involve constricted, rigid thinking patterns, and all-or-nothing thinking. The autistic brain is great at homing in and sustaining attention to detail. This is fine when your child is focused on a useful special interest. It becomes a hindrance, though, if your child has anxiety or depression. When they face an obstacle, their brain tends to fixate on it, and that is worse if they're in a bad mood. When people are depressed or anxious, whether autistic or not, their thinking becomes less flexible.

If your child is stuck in chronic negative thinking, suspect depression. If their language, drawings, or video games have repeated themes of darkness and death, take it as a warning sign. Get yourself in a grounded state of mind and calmly ask them to tell you more. Ask them about the drawings from a place of genuine curiosity. Ask about the characters in their video games—why they do what they do, and what their missions are. For now, just listen. Don't negate your child's experience by telling them they shouldn't feel a certain way. Instead, praise their honesty. Tell them you are glad they told you what they were thinking.

When your child is depressed, they ignore and discount the positive. It's as though their brain is magnetically drawn to dark thoughts. While teens in general often struggle with existential questions about life's meaning, they typically have enough activities, responsibilities, and relationships to give their lives context and value. As they increasingly clarify and refine their identity, they usually find growing satisfaction with their day-to-day lives.

But an autistic teen struggling with isolation or lack of meaningful activities in their daily life has no foundation for this growth. If this describes your child, you must help them make concrete lifestyle changes to fight their isolation and emptiness. With the help of a therapist experienced in working with autistic teens, or at least guided by self-help books, you also need to introduce specific cognitive, behavioral, and physical interventions to combat depression and anxiety. We'll walk you through examples later in this chapter.

But First: Are You Struggling, Too?

Parents raising children on the spectrum are often struggling, too. There are many studies showing higher depression rates in families with autistic children. Numbers vary, but at least one study found that about 50% of parents had been actually been diagnosed with a depressive disorder prior to the birth of their child with autism. If you didn't start out depressed, years of battling for your child may have exhausted you and contributed to an onset of depression.

Parents preparing their children and teens for adulthood need energy, optimism, and a clear mind. Left untreated, depression in a parent can hamper your child's successful transition to adulthood. Heed the advice of the airlines: Put on your own oxygen mask before your child's!

If you suspect depression or an anxiety problem, start by going online and doing a search using the terms depression and/or anxiety and "screening." Don't substitute it for a real diagnosis, but it's a start. Print it out if possible and take it to your family doctor.

Environmental Factors You Can't Overlook

Isolation and inactivity contribute greatly to mood disorders. Your child needs interaction with others and the good feeling that comes from mastering tasks. Without these two experiences, almost anyone is at risk for becoming anxious or depressed. It's a vicious downward spiral. A teen that has struggled with autism has often internalized a negative self-concept. If no one actively engages them in the world, they may retreat into a limited, narrow life. This life probably won't have any tasks that give them a sense of self-pride. So they are left with just the constant internal replaying of negative self-talk. Consequently, their self-image further deteriorates, and they become more mired in isolation and desolation.

You must find the determination, strength, and help to push your child out of this cycle. We can't emphasize enough that they cannot be expected to do it themselves. We've devoted an entire chapter later in this book to life skills you have to help your child with, because it is so critical.

You Can Change Your Child's Poor Sleep Habits

Parents often know about but don't intervene in their teen's sleep habits. Therapists also often fail to address this. If your child is in counseling, be sure you give their therapist detailed information about their sleep patterns.

Your child needs regular and sufficient nighttime sleep cycles. Sleep problems are common in children and teens with autism, and create many secondary problems. Sleep is a central biological mechanism that determines our body's ability to function well. Sleep regulates and impacts mood, learning, memory, body sensations, and our sensory reactions, immune systems, and behaviors.

Many studies show that ASD children and teens are negatively impacted in serious ways if they don't get enough sleep, or if they sleep during the day instead of at night. Studies have found that fewer hours of sleep are correlated with more social skills deficits, more stereotyped behaviors, greater sensory challenges, higher rates of oppositional behavior and aggression, and a greater rate of ADHD and other psychiatric diagnoses. They've also found negative impact on cognitive abilities, such as impaired ability to concentrate, and even lower IQ scores. In one study, sleep problems were the number one predictor of challenging behaviors in ASD.

Your child's sleep patterns can be improved by using basic sleep hygiene strategies. First, you may need to make changes to their patterns before bedtime Lights from electronic devices such as computers, tablets, and cell phones should be turned off an hour or two before going to bed. The light from these devices has a short wavelength. This type of light shuts down your child's natural production of melatonin, a hormone they need to bring on sleep. Normally, melatonin naturally starts to rise about two hours before natural bedtimes. It tells our bodies to shut down for the night so we can recover from the day's energy drain and recharge by the next morning.

Teen brains are especially vulnerable to the light from electronics. An hour of exposure before bedtime decreases their melatonin by 23%, and two hours brings it down almost 40%. Less melatonin throws off your child's circadian clock. It also reduces their REM sleep, which is the kind of sleep that restores their energy. Without it, they wake up groggy and in a bad mood.

Your child should also avoid daytime napping. During the day, they need to go outside and get exposed to light, even if it's a cloudy day.

Other Sleep Wreckers

Food close to bedtime and anything that stimulates your kid's brain and body interferes with good sleep. This includes any kind of caffeine, whether in coffee, tea, sodas, energy drinks, flavored water, or chocolate. Some over-the-counter pain relievers have lots of caffeine, too.

Many teens on the spectrum have gotten into the habit of regarding their bedroom as their entire world. These teens have trained their brains to associate their bed with arousal (TV, video gaming, Internet) instead of rest and sleep. Get them back into the living room in the evening, unless they are reading in bed and that helps them fall asleep.

Use these strategies every single night for a month. If sleep is still impaired, consider researching melatonin supplements or other over-the-counter sleep aids. Melatonin tends to have a mildly helpful effect, but some people report side effects of headaches and daytime sleepiness. Most other over-the-counter sleep aids contain antihistamines, and tolerance to their sedative effects can develop quickly. Supplements made from valerian are also sometimes taken as sleep aids. Studies of their effectiveness seem mixed.

What to Do When Your Teen Loves Junk Food

Poor diet can contribute to poor mood. We realize you've heard this before, and your teen probably loves to eat junk food (otherwise known as crap). But whereas your neurotypical adolescent might get away with an unhealthy diet, a teen with autism has more to lose. Their preference for sameness means that whatever habits they've developed by the time they reach adolescence are likely the habits they'll hold on to forever. And once they're on their own, it's out of your hands. Now is the time to make changes.

What do we mean by junk food? Obviously fast food counts, since it's high in fat, calories, sugar, salt, and additives. The manufacturers of fast food spent tons of money conducting research to see how to make their products the most addicting. Explain this to your children and ask them if they really want corporations "duping" them like that. Kids on the spectrum are logical and hate manipulation, so make sure they understand that's what the junk food industry is all about. Some of them will care about this.

Other foods are crap, too, but less obvious. Most processed foods qualify. Teach your teen to read labels and show them that many products come in lower sodium options (soups and canned goods in general). Explain to your kid that grocery stores put their healthier foods along the perimeter of the stores (fruits, vegetables, whole grains, proteins) and the processed foods in the middle. Tell them to buy most of their groceries from the outer aisles of the store.

Breakfast is a Danger Zone

Breakfast is a real danger zone for many kids on the spectrum, especially if they sleep late—they awake famished and grab whatever is easiest. Almost all boxed cereals are loaded with sugar, and on an empty stomach will probably spike your kid's blood sugar levels. They briefly feel good, then their energy and mood crash. Get the stuff out of the house. Explain to your kid why you're ditching the cereal, and again include the fact that the food industry relies on consumers being uninformed (or, in your kid's words, "stupid"). Put them in a logical bind. Ask them why they would let strangers make money off their ignorance when they are smarter than that.

Remember, your teen won't learn about healthy food choices magically. You need to teach them. You also need to teach them how to shop. A good webpage to review together is www.everydayhealth.com, which has a section called "Guide to Grocery Shopping."

Your child isn't likely to take the lead in changing their diet. If you're financially supporting your teen, you have a lot of control over what they eat. Stop buying what you know is bad. They'll complain, but it's unlikely they're going to start shopping on their own. Start with whatever unhealthy foods have become habitual, and don't bring them into the house. If your teen leaves the house and spends your money on fast food, it's time to take back the privilege of unassigned spending money.

The habit of irregular, poor diet goes beyond health consequences. If they're living at home, but not eating dinner at the table with the family, they're also missing important opportunities for honing practical and social skills.

To Change Their Mood, Get Your Kid Moving!

Lots of kids and teens on the spectrum are in bad physical shape. They might have come into the world with poor muscle tone or developed it from not using their bodies. Some spectrum kids tend to be uncoordinated. That, combined with social deficits and lack of interest, often kept them away from organized sports. In years past, these same kids may have gotten exercise just running around the neighborhood and exploring. But this generation, especially kids on the spectrum, often spend their childhood sitting in front of a screen.

A sedentary lifestyle correlates highly with poor health in general and with mood disorders in particular. You don't need to get your teen to a gym (although if they do, some young adults on the spectrum make it a routine and then never miss a workout). Instead of thinking "exercise," think "movement."

We know exercise and movement has tons of benefits. When we get moving, our body increases the number of our insulin receptors, which means we use our blood glucose better and our cells grow stronger. We don't just get toned; we literally get a whole body tune-up.

Aerobic exercise calms the body's stress reaction down. It works both for those who suffer from actual anxiety disorders as well as the average person with day-to-day stress. It also improves people's mood, and British doctors now use it as a first-line treatment for depression. Tons of parents also swear that exercise helps their kids focus better.

Martha described how she regularly needs the calming that comes from what she calls "*heavy lifting.*" She emphasized that first she has to be sure to handle any sensory issues in order for depression and anxiety to stay under control. Once that's taken care of, she finds that periodic heavy work (lifting heavy items, moving furniture, that sort of thing) refreshes and calms her. She combines that with lots of down time on weekends, when she listens to music, plays with her cat, or just relaxes. She says the combination provides stability and recovery from life's stress.

Exercise also fights addictions. Researchers have found that even five minutes of intense exercise helps. In smokers, even this small amount of exercise held off cravings for a cigarette for 50 minutes. When people exercise, they start making better decisions about other behaviors too. They eat healthier, lose their temper less often, and drink less caffeine and alcohol. Even newborns of exercising moms vs. non-exercising moms seem to benefit. They were more responsive to stimuli and better able to quiet themselves down after being disturbed by a sensory irritation (sound or light). This has profound implications for those on the spectrum with sensory struggles.

They Don't Have to Love It—They Just Have to Do It!

Invite your teen to walk with you. Start small and go somewhere they enjoy, preferably in nature. You may be pleasantly surprised that during these walks they relax and open up. Conversation often flows better when you are beside your child and moving, rather than facing them and stationary.

Once autistic kids get into a habit, they do great at maintaining it. Help them apply this to movement or exercise. Make a chart or put notes on a calendar until the schedule becomes a rule. They don't have to like the activity; they just have to see the benefit and logic of it.

Temple does 100 sit-ups every night before going to bed. She does not like doing them. In fact, she HATES doing them! But she knows they have to be done if she wants to sleep well.

Pain and Inflammation Can Cause Mood Disorders

Underlying conditions such as pain or inflammation can produce secondary mood disorders. Kids with autism often have more issues with gut problems, and these are often unrecognized or untreated. Ask your child or teen if they have stomach or bowel upset. They may not think to tell you. If present, successful treatment of these disorders can have an immediate effect on mood.

Addressing Psychological Issues: Counseling and Other Approaches

The right therapist or coach can help your child, but is no substitute for your active involvement and loving pushes. A 50 minute weekly appointment is nothing compared to how much time you spend with your child. Also, beware of traditional talk therapies that rely on insight and your child's attachment to the therapist as the primary ingredients in treatment. This doesn't work for most adolescents on the spectrum. These kids instead require logic-based reasoning (not just emotional support), consistently combined with a concrete action plan.

A therapist who understands autism will also realize that the usual confidentiality restrictions between teen and parent need to be modified. They'll welcome your participation in treatment and need you to be their eyes and ears at home between appointments. While there will still be some confidences not shared with you, you should be asked to sign an authorization for at least limited communication between you and the therapist.

It's highly likely that you, not your teen or young adult, are paying for the therapy. You are making a substantial financial sacrifice for your child's benefit. You want to make that sacrifice worth it, so it is a reasonable request for you to require conditions most conducive to success.

Cognitive Behavioral Therapy (CBT) & How It's Used

Cognitive behavioral therapy is the intervention that's been found most effective for those diagnosed with autism and a mood disorder. A therapist with this approach examines the relationships between a person's thoughts, feelings, and behaviors. They help clients reduce emotional pain by showing them how their feelings are often linked to distorted negative thoughts. When your child learns what their automatic "self-talk" is, they can observe it from a distance and begin to question its truth. Many children on the spectrum have always been hyperaware of anything they see as negative, but they aren't aware of how skewed their perceptions are.

CBT therapists help clients identify their specific triggers for depressive or fearful thoughts. Your child probably judges him or herself harshly, and they may be ashamed of parts of themselves. By voicing these thoughts, your child diminishes their power. CBT therapists teach clients that thoughts are not facts. CBT does not require extensive self-reflection or recognition of emotional or social nuance. The therapist is an active, engaged participant, not a passive listener.

CBT therapists move beyond exploring thoughts and feelings. They actively work with clients to develop concrete behavior changes. The approach is structured. They may assign homework (in which case your participation may be requested) that involves practicing new behaviors. The client then reports back on any obstacles they encountered, and adjustments are made to the assignment with these in mind. Then they practice again the next week, and keep this up until they are able to eliminate all obstacles and achieve success with the new behavior.

"Mindfulness" Can Prevent Negativity From Grabbing Hold of Your Child

Teaching a skill called "mindfulness" is frequently included in CBT therapy. You may come across therapists who refer to themselves as MBCT (Mindfulness Based Cognitive Therapy) practitioners. These therapists help clients learn to pay close attention to what they are experiencing in a given moment. This includes body sensations such as breath or muscle tightness, as well as thoughts and feelings. The goal is to quickly recognize and name experiences *before* stress and negative states take hold. This form of therapy has proven effective in reducing both depression and anxiety, and increasing positive emotions in young adults with autism.

When your child's stress is reduced, he is able to concentrate and focus better and his moods become more stable. It is easier for someone to communicate and relate to others when stress is under control. Physical health benefits from stress reduction, and your child also has a greater feeling of control.

No Access to a Therapist? You Can Still Use These Strategies!

CBT is not rocket science. Don't let the big name scare you off. If you don't have access to a therapist, parents, teachers, ministers, or others can still use CBT and mindfulness with your child. Start, like all good therapists, by being genuine, respectful of the child's struggles, and supportive of their strengths. Be an "active listener." Let them voice their thoughts without interrupting or judging. Then follow up by asking questions so you understand even more about their experience. This will also help them clarify their thoughts and feelings.

Here is what *not* to do. Don't tell a child "everything will be okay," or "just stop worrying," or "be more positive." They are empty platitudes. A child needs concrete guidelines and steps. Also, don't tell them to "stop thinking" about something. That's like someone telling you to not think of a "red alligator." It actually directs your mind there—your brain automatically pictures a red alligator.

Tell the child you're going to help them figure out what they want to change, and that together you will take steps to make these changes. First, define the problem. It has to be specific; "I am unhappy" or "No one likes me" is not specific enough. Take your time with this first step, or you'll sabotage the results. If the child says they're unhappy, make them explain *what* things they are unhappy about, and then name the most important source of unhappiness and work on that first. Tackle one thing at a time. A good example would be "I am unhappy that I do not have a job."

This is an appropriate target because it is concrete, specific, and measurable. You either have a job or you don't (although you always want to break it down as specifically as possible, so in this example, you have to find out if a "job" includes volunteer, non-paying work, or part-time work). Here's where setting goals comes in. You and the child write down the problem, and then you write down the goal.

Then you brainstorm together and write down all of your ideas. You can eliminate some later. For now, just write down everything. Then select a small step that will take the child closer to the goal. For example, "I will look at the job ads each morning at 9:00 AM and write down any that I could do." If the child isn't ready for that, then you figure out what is realistic and write that down. It might be, "I will Google volunteer opportunities in our town and write down at least two I would try." If even that is too much (and it may be if a child has not gained any confidence or skills because they haven't even had "jobs" around the house), then a step might be "I will learn to (fill in the blank—maybe do laundry, cook dinner, mow the lawn) to increase my basic skills in preparation for a real job in the future."

After you define the goal, you must track progress toward it in writing. Set a specific time each day to sit down with your child; otherwise, it won't happen. If the step was not done, brainstorm why. Did fear get in the way? Did he think he would fail? Did he "forget" to do it? Trying new things doesn't usually go smoothly, so expect these types of issues. Instead of giving up, go back a step and brainstorm the reason for the obstacle. You and the child have to be detectives and learn everything you can about what interfered with doing the step.

Make a list of all the thoughts and beliefs that are obstacles. Examples might be "No one would hire me," or "I don't know how to interview," or "I'm too slow." Identify these as "automatic thoughts" that you need to take a closer, logic-based look at. Ask the child what "proof" they have of the truth of these thoughts. Walk through this "proof" with disputing evidence. If there are obstacles that are realistic, come up with a plan to address them. If the child really has no clue how to interview, he's right; that's an obstacle that needs working on first. Keep breaking down the obstacles until the distorted ones are replaced with realistic thoughts and the realistic ones are removed or lessened. If you haven't already, get others involved at this step—extended family, friendly neighbors, ministers, and teachers are all great people to enlist so that a child has a variety of support.

When you can't get past obstacles, you may need to help your child learn techniques to reduce their anxiety and increase their confidence. To reduce anxiety, go back to the basics and make sure they are under control (sleep, movement, diet). Make sure your child's sensory environment is not overwhelming. Then try one or both of the following strategies.

Two Easy-to-Teach Relaxation and Mindfulness Techniques (for Your Child and for You!)

You can teach your child two standard relaxation techniques (and practice them yourself, too). One is "belly breathing," and goes like this: have your child either sit comfortably, or lie down on their back. If they are comfortable closing their eyes, have them do it. That way they aren't distracted by you or anything else they can see. Tell them to put one hand over their heart, and the other hand over their belly. Have them breathe in at a relaxed pace to the count of five, and then back out, again to the count of five. The goal is to breathe all the way down into their belly instead of just up in their chest. They can tell if that's happening by which hand is moving up and down as they breathe. If it's the one on their chest, have them keep trying until they can switch it to the hand on their belly. Tell them not to forcefully push their stomach out, but just let their breath do it. Tell them not to expect a dramatic movement, just a gentle rise and fall of their belly. Do it with them until they (and you) get the hang of it. Teach your other kids—make it a family activity. Debra's counseling practice worked with one child who didn't want to learn this, but once invited to show her little sister, she relished the "teacher" role, and proudly brought her to therapy to demonstrate how well it had went. Of course, in the meantime, she'd learned the technique herself.

The second standard mindfulness tool you can teach is called progressive relaxation. You teach your child to first tense, and then relax, a series of muscle groups. The goal is for them to become aware of any tension in their body and learn to let it go. Lots of ASD kids have chronic muscle tension and don't even realize it.

Again, this is a good family exercise and something that everyone can benefit from. First, get in a comfortable position. Then have everyone start with the bottom of the body and move up ("feet to forehead"). Tense each muscle group and hold it for about five seconds, then release it and feel the difference. Enjoy the sensation for about 15 seconds, and then move to the next muscle group. You can pick and choose muscle groups to do, but usually you'll first curl your toes, then tighten your calf muscles by pulling your toes up, then squeeze your thigh muscles. You can do one side of the body at a time or both.

Then move on to the buttocks (squeeze them together), the stomach (suck it in), the chest (take a deep, tight chest breath—not a belly one), and the neck and shoulders (raise your shoulders to your ears).

Then do your arms, first clenching and then relaxing each fist, and then the biceps (making a "Popeye" muscle). Finally, tense and relax your face. Open your mouth wide enough to feel a stretch, then let it gently close. Then clench your eyes shut, and then gently open them. And finally, tense your forehead by raising your eyebrows as high as you can, then letting them relax. Remember to enjoy the feeling of relaxation for each step before moving on to the next muscle group. Don't rush the exercise.

You can also Google these steps so you can print them out, and there are lots of CDs you can purchase at your bookstore or online to guide you through the steps.

They often have relaxing soft music in the background. If your library carries CDs, they may have one with these exercises.

Animals Can Reinforce Mindfulness

Some individuals on the autism spectrum find that animals are sources of comfort. Trained service animals can alert them to changes in their internal emotional state before they themselves become aware of it. Then the person can start using strategies to regain emotional and sensory relief. If you can't afford or don't have access to a trained service animal, just get an ordinary pet. Pick one that has a gentle nature and doesn't startle easily.

Sarah has a service dog that provides one of several good ways she copes with her anxiety.

> I struggle with anxiety, and I have a couple of ways that I cope with it and they have helped. I currently have a service dog that helps me to see when I am anxious. I then use breathing techniques to try to relax. Therapy has facilitated me to learn to slow down and think about gaining order and control of myself. I also wear earplugs in areas with excessive auditory input. The HBO film *Temple Grandin* was essential in relieving me of any shame about my difference and in allowing me to accept myself. The film also demonstrated coping skills for anxiety, sensory, and lack of confidence issues. I realized that I, like Temple with her squeeze machine, wanted to have a feeling of being held by something predictable and controllable. One coping strategy I use for my anxiety is wearing tight jeans or fitted shoes, or placing my hands on my stomach or lower back. Unknowingly, I held my breath when anxious but knew that the pressure technique helped me because my breath becomes normal after having the pressure that an object or I myself provided. The reliable tactile feeling comforted me.

Numerous other therapies, both mainstream and less so, have been helpful for some people with anxiety or depression. Daniel's mother recalled that high doses of the over-the-counter dietary supplement SAM-e made a significant difference for her son after one particularly difficult bout with depression. Occupational therapy is fairly commonly used for sensory challenges and often helps reduce anxiety. A meta-analysis of nine studies of music therapy concluded it had consistent positive effects for those with autism. Other parents and children have found a variety of alternate ways to combat anxiety and sensory overload. One mom, Michelle, whose daughter "Suzanne" is not profiled here and wants to remain anonymous, found that massage, music, and essential oils helped alleviate her daughter's anxiety when she was a child. She still uses these aides and has also added yoga and meditation as an adult.

Group Support for Children, Teens, and Parents

Both CBT and mindfulness therapy can also be done in small groups. Many individuals with autism, though, resist group therapy. They often say they "know" they won't like the other participants. Beneath this apparent contempt is usually fear. It's understandable that group therapy is viewed as just another social encounter likely to end in feeling different, unaccepted, and weird. Your child needs to be told that group meetings for those on the spectrum take a practical approach—they're not about exploring relationships between group members, which most teens with autism find boring or irrelevant.

Many communities now have informal meetings for teens and young adults on the autism spectrum. A good place to find them is on the huge website www.meetup.com. Once you get to the site, search for a group by entering your location and the word autism or Asperger's. These groups are often led by trained therapists, but sometimes by a parent or other layperson. They are usually free or charge only a nominal fee, and are usually drop in (which takes the pressure off). They tend to meet once a month on average. Members are usually incredibly supportive of each other. The groups vary in focus—a few offer social outings, others are more educational, or just a place to talk about common challenges and to share successes. They are not a substitute for treatment, but they're definitely therapeutic. If your community doesn't have one, look at ones in other towns and consider starting your own, modeled on one you like the looks of.

Jaime and Sarah have both participated in groups off and on and found them helpful. Jaime's comments are a typical reaction.

Whether you've been formally diagnosed or not, in either case it's a very, very good way to meet others that are like oneself. And that in and of itself is HUGE. We don't just feel like outcasts. We are outcasts. Our brain wiring is different, and once we're able to connect to others like us it is so comforting. It's like a big hug.

Groups for parents are out there too, and can be a tremendous source of support and education. Dawn, mother of an adult daughter diagnosed with Asperger's, found great relief when she attended.

Once my daughter was diagnosed, it was suggested that I attend a support group and I went to several, but mostly they were for adults with Asperger's and that was not too helpful. I finally found a group for parents—and it was the first time in over 23 years that I felt someone understood—finally someone got me. I had only just met them but they were truly kindred spirits. I didn't have to try to explain myself or defend myself. It was the best day I had in a long time. I would highly recommend that to every parent.

Both depression and anxiety can also be successfully treated in more targeted weekly therapy groups. These usually focus on specific areas like social skills or vocational preparation. Again, most participants join only if pushed by parents. But once they join, few drop out. It is worth the push. Being in a small group of like-minded peers is powerful. They know what it feels like to be bullied, to struggle to fit in, and to be challenged by anxiety and dark moods.

You may have read older literature saying people on the autism spectrum lack empathy. We now know this is wrong. You probably realize that your child has plenty of empathy when they can read and "get" a situation that calls for it. They may not care about the same things NT youth care about, but when they do care, it is often intensely. Therapists who have led groups for those with autism can attest to this. Even though they may have resisted in the beginning, most group members naturally develop caring and empathy for the other members.

Psychotherapy Approaches Not Recommended

You should be aware of two other commonly used therapy approaches that are not recommended for those with autism. Neither tends to work well, because they rely on ways of thinking and relating that do not come naturally for individuals with autism. We recommend you interview prospective therapists and screen them to find out if they really understand the autistic brain and if their therapeutic approach is a good fit for it.

One of the non-recommended approaches goes by the terms "person-centered" (PCT) or "client-centered," or "supportive" therapy. This was developed by psychologist Carl Rogers, and is still sometimes referred to as Rogerian therapy. This approach does work well for some NT clients. It's less likely to help those on the spectrum because it relies heavily on self-initiation, assumes the client has theory of mind, and does not impose a structure on the therapy. Individuals on the autism spectrum need guidance and prodding to create structure and goals. They usually flounder without this supportive push from outside.

The other therapeutic approach not recommended is known as psychodynamic or "insight oriented" therapy. Focusing on bringing unconscious thoughts and feelings into awareness, the therapist with this approach helps their client closely examine both past and present conflicts. This form of therapy assumes that most symptoms result from maladaptive, unconscious roles that were adopted in childhood and now, as they continue into adulthood, sabotage healthy functioning. While those with autism may certainly have old and unhealthy ways of thinking and behaving, they usually need a more active, direct approach in order to make changes.

The Therapist's Personality and Surroundings

A teen or young adult with autism frequently prefers that their therapist have certain personality traits. They highly value intelligence and straight talk. They do best with a therapist who can laugh and be irreverent in their humor, and who genuinely appreciates their client's quirks and special interests. They usually don't do well with long, rambling explanations or with silence. They usually dislike excessive praise. They are often intolerant of therapists who do not start and stop precisely on time. Appointments should be scheduled, at least at the beginning, on the same day of each week, at the same time. (Later in therapy, changing it up occasionally can be a way of helping your child learn to adjust to change.)

The conditions of the therapy and waiting room are also very important. The office should be well insulated against outside noise. Other sensory issues should be considered as well. Most spectrum clients dislike candles (other clients often love the ambience, but clients with autism may find them distracting or have a bad reaction to their scent). Lamps or filtered natural light are preferable to fluorescent lights. Spinning ceiling fans are distracting and may even bring on headaches. Seating should allow options; two chairs directly across from each other in close proximity won't work. These are environmental aspects your child might never think to tell you about, but they can ruin their therapy experience.

Tips about Medication

The benefits of your child's counseling may be greatly augmented by adding medication. We're not "pro" or "con" medication—sometimes it's a lifesaver, sometimes there seems to be no effect, and sometimes side effects outweigh the benefits. We want to emphasize that we are not suggesting autism itself needs treating. We are saying that the depression and anxiety that often occur alongside autism may be helped by medication.

We do believe too many kids are not getting the relief medications can provide. We also believe too many kids are getting the wrong kinds of medications that are too strong, too risky, and given out way too liberally. Psychiatrists (and pediatric neurologists) have increasingly used second-generation antipsychotics "off label" with children and teens with autism, even though they have no psychotic symptoms. Documented risk factors include sedation, diabetes, heart disease, higher levels of prolactin, and weight gain. If your doctor wants to prescribe this type of drug, do your research, and consider getting a second opinion before you make your decision.

The first-line medications for depression, as well as anxiety and panic, are usually various antidepressants known as SSRIs (selective serotonin reuptake inhibitors). Commonly used ones include Prozac (Fluoxetine), Zoloft (Sertraline), and Celexa (Citalopram), but there are others also. While this category of drugs is called antidepressants, they are routinely used for anxiety, so don't let the term confuse you. Another class of drugs, benzodiazepines, are also used to treat anxiety, but are sedating, which can be a problem for some people. They can also cause physical dependence and withdrawal if used long term. For those reasons, they are often avoided if possible, used only short term, or used in their lowest effective dose as a supplement to an SSRI.

Antidepressants don't take effect right away. They often take at least a few weeks to kick in. Patience is required, because complete effect may not even occur for several months. Benzodiazepines, on the other hand, kick in quicker, but still vary in how long it takes to feel their effects. The usual range of peak effect is anywhere from just under an hour to four hours.

You may also want to research probiotics, which are live microorganisms that when administered in adequate amounts, provide a health benefit. There is research that in addition to changing the composition of bacteria in the gut (and helping various stomach and bowel issues), these over-the-counter aids also lower anxiety. We know that there are many serotonin receptors in our gut, so perhaps we can improve mood problems not only via the brain, but also via the stomach. This is a new approach, and your doctor may not be aware of the studies on probiotics and anxiety. We've included some articles in the reference section for you to share with them.

Start Slow—Many Autistic People are Extra Sensitive to Medication

Autistic individuals can be very sensitive to medication, so it is wise to start with lower than typical doses. Parents must very closely monitor mood and behavior once medication is started. Keeping a list of reactions helps. Note any changes in sleep, appetite, energy, agitation, anxiety, depressed mood, pessimistic or optimistic statements, and what your child is mainly talking about. Report them to the prescribing doctor—do not rely on your teen to do this. If a medication is stopped, it is VERY important that it is done gradually, tapering it down very slowly to avoid withdrawal problems that may include increased anxiety or even seizures.

By definition, autism is a spectrum disorder and there are probably countless varieties of subtypes not yet identified or understood. Even psychiatrists who specialize in autism are on a learning curve about which medications and doses work best for those on the autism spectrum. You might be lucky and the first medication you try works great, but you might have to try a few before you find the right drug and dosage. Give the medication a fair trial—remember that SSRIs can take months to reach 100% of their eventual effect. Folks often quit too early and think the medication didn't help, when it just hadn't had enough time to work.

It's critically important that both parents and psychologists or other providers working with your child give extensive input to prescribing physicians. If the physician doesn't want this input, go somewhere else. Selecting an appropriate medication requires obtaining a comprehensive profile of your child, and you want them to have as much input as possible. The doctor should obtain a good family and medical history, learn details of current behaviors and symptoms, and know about past responses to medications.

If a thorough diagnostic evaluation hasn't been done prior to starting medication, you've skipped a step. "Eyeballing" your child is not valid diagnosing, but it happens. Today's psychiatrists are swamped—it's the least popular and most poorly paid field of medicine, so there aren't enough to go around. (Medical procedures bring in the money; psychiatrists don't tend to do procedures.) So realize it will fall to you to prepare for your child's appointment. Take a printout (not handwritten!) of bullet points you want the psychiatrist to know. No sentences, just bullet points. Seriously, their time is super limited—be smart and work with it. Consider faxing it the day before (not earlier—old faxes tend to get lost), but always bring a copy with you to personally hand over at the beginning of the appointment.

How to Involve Your Teen So You're Not Wasting Your Time

Involve your teen with this process. Make them sit down with you when you're preparing the bullet point list. It's often really helpful to have a family session with their therapist just a few days before the psychiatrist appointment. Walk through in detail the reasons for taking the medication and what you want it to help. Do not appeal to your child's emotions or try to guilt them. Appeal to their logical mind that wants relief.

Reassure your child that this is a trial, not a commitment—they need to clearly hear from you that if the medicine doesn't work, or if there are intolerable side effects, it will be stopped. Listen carefully to any concerns your child has about taking medicine and don't offer platitudes. If you don't have answers to their concerns, go online and try to find them, and write them on your list also.

Compliance with medication can be an issue. There are three things you can do to minimize this problem. First, as just mentioned, get your kid involved from the start and give them facts. Second, emphasize that they must give it a fair trial, and give them realistic time frames for their particular medication to take effect. If your child doesn't have this information from the beginning, they may give up too soon. Third, make it easy for your child to remember to take the medicine. Put it somewhere highly visible (don't hide it or keep it a secret from siblings old enough to understand). Make sure it is taken at the same time every day. Pick a time you know you can monitor, at least at the beginning. Obviously your child will need to manage their medication on their own when they achieve independence, but for now, most will need your reminders. Have your child check off when they take the medicine each day. A small note pad held around the pill bottle by a rubber band works well.

Expect more frequent visits to the psychiatrist at the beginning. Usually they will be once a week. Appointments will usually be spaced out later, after symptoms show improvement and any side effects are eliminated. But if you observe changes before the next scheduled appointment, do not wait. Call and at least get on a cancellation wait list if no appointments are available.

Depression and anxiety do not have to be disabling adjuncts to autism. Acknowledge them, treat them, and use all the tools at your disposal. Parents and professionals may have to apply many "loving pushes" before a teen agrees to get help, but in the end it is worth it.

> I was depressed and anxious most of my life. I used to cope mainly by withdrawing into my fantasy world. But as an adult I have taken advantage of therapy. I also take medication. Fortunately, I am on Lexapro (Escitalopram) now and that has helped me a lot. I also take Tegretol (Carbamazepine), which helps cut down some of the sensory challenges. And my goal is always to improve my diet, exercise, and relaxation routines, because I do feel better when I am able to stick to them.
>
> – Martha, 57

CHAPTER 6

DANGER AHEAD:
Compulsive Gaming and
Media Recluses

Every time Temple gives a talk, desperate moms come up to her asking how to get their son out of the bedroom and off video games. Debra, too, found compulsive gaming was a problem in the majority of her male ASD clients. So while this chapter may or may not describe your child, there are many families who are being greatly impacted by video gaming and we're betting you know at least one. Please share this information with them even if it does not affect your own child. You could make a big difference in the quality of another family's life.

We now know that children, teens, and adults on the autism spectrum are extra-vulnerable to becoming fixated on screen-based media. Compulsive use ruins educational, social, and vocational development. Males are the most vulnerable, and way too many boys and men on the spectrum have become online recluses in their bedrooms. They identify more with online activities than the real world. Young women are less likely to play video games, and when they do, they spend about 50% less time on them. They also seem, like Cosette, to prefer games involving animals or puzzles, or like Marina, use the Internet primarily for researching diverse interests.

In this chapter we'll tell you how gaming affects your child's brain, why autistic kids are especially vulnerable, how game developers intentionally construct games to create compulsion-ripe conditions, and what you must do if your child has been sucked in. And if your child has not been seduced by gaming, we'll help you keep it that way.

Before we discuss how to reclaim your child, we are going to tell you about gaming and what happens behind the scenes. That's because we want you to really "get" what this epidemic is about, and we want you to be well informed so you can protect and help your child. The earlier you start the better, but it's never too late. The brain is capable of change at any age, but if your child has developed a gaming compulsion, they will need a *very strong* loving push from you.

Each of the individuals profiled in this book has had some involvement with online activities. With the exception of Martha, who is in her late 50s and says she's "not of that generation," all of them have played online games. Most of the males played extensively. Even Martha, though, says she has a hard time staying off the social media site Facebook.

> I feel as though I could do a lot of other things that are more productive or relaxing, but Facebook and news online or via radio can be very addicting. I can spend too much time online at work instead of doing my assignments. And at home, if I spend more than half an hour on Facebook I never fail to lift my head without feeling disappointed that I gave up so much of my personal time on something that is so inherently unfulfilling.

Others can become fixated on their favorite TV shows, and refuse to leave the house when they are on (and refuse to tape them for later viewing). Some become stuck in endless loops of Internet surfing that produce no useful results and keep them from productive endeavors. Any screen activity that becomes a compulsion and interferes with real life is a problem that parents need to address. We're focusing on compulsive gaming in this book, because in our experience it's the main problem. There has been very little research comparing video game usage of NT and ASD children, but what has been done tells us we are in big trouble. We need to take strong steps to prevent compulsive gaming in our kids.

Terms You Need to Know as a Parent

"Genres" are categories of video games based on *how the player* interacts with the game. Some genres cause more problems for kids than others. Common genres include first person shooter, action, adventure, action-adventure (which adds stealth or survival elements), simulation (where the player constructs and manages a simulated environment or vehicle), strategy (often associated with military strategy), sports, puzzles, or specific card, word, or board games.

Within these genres, games can be played alone, or simultaneously with up to 10,000 players from around the world. When large numbers of players are involved, the term *MMOG* (massively multiplayer online [role-playing] game) is used. This has become a *tremendously* popular and problematic kind of game. MMOG games never end, and players can interact with them, and with each other, at any hour of the day or night.

MMOG players are in a real time world of amazing, highly stimulating 3D graphics. They create and customize a personal "avatar," their character that interacts with the environment and other players. Your child gets to select *many* detailed characteristics for this persona—everything from gender, race, skin tone, age, height and weight, build, facial features, eye color and shape, hair color and style, and body markings like freckles or tattoos. They also decide their character's profession, personality, weaknesses and strengths, and beliefs. They can buy special powers for their avatar.

Since MMOG games have no ending, your child never reaches an ultimate "win." They are constantly presented with almost limitless choices of content and strategies. Once they master one level, they immediately advance to another. New versions of the games come out all the time. *EverQuest*, one of the most popular games, boasts the following on its website:

- Experience 18 years of continuous development including 21 expansions of amazing content
- Build your character through 100 levels of power
- More than 500 zones to explore
- Thousands of Alternate Abilities available to further customize your character
- More than 50,000 items to earn and collect

The 50,000 items they refer to *are not free* to your child. "Free-to-play" games (usually just written as F2P) give players access to part of the game without initially paying. This model became popular in early MMOGs, and can be very expensive to players and highly profitable to developers. Your child doesn't have to spend lots of money, but you should know that there are annual worldwide conferences devoted just to gaming "monetization," strategies to keep your child spending money once they start playing. For example, your child may have to pay to add cosmetic characteristics to their avatar or to the game, or to give their avatar more power, or to speed up how fast they can progress in the game. Developers may put a time limit on the item purchased. After a certain amount of time, the item disappears, and the gamer has to pay to get it again. Critics of these games call them *"pay-to-win"* games, since gamers unwilling to pay for special items may fall behind other players. Your child has to continually pay up to keep up.

Your child probably isn't in a position to have the money to buy all the bells and whistles now. But you have to wonder if they will have the judgment not to do it once they are independent and have an income.

Games Where Your Child Builds or Creates Things

Another genre of video games is virtual building games such as Minecraft. In this game, elaborate structures can be built from blocks manipulated on the computer. Many parents have told Temple that their child is spending way too much time playing Minecraft. Fortunately, excessive Minecraft use may be easier to direct into more constructive activities than the multiplayer games. Minecraft runs on Java Script, and it can be used as a gateway for learning computer programming. There are many job opportunities for people who are good Java Script coders.

One innovative mom directed her child's interest in Minecraft into activities with other children playing with wooden blocks. She had a bunch of blocks cut from boards at a lumberyard. The next step was to have the neighborhood kids and her son paint them with the Minecraft color scheme. Her son with autism became a big hit in the neighborhood. Many kids came over to play with the wooden Minecraft blocks in the driveway of their home. This is a good example of taking an interest in an online activity and directing it into a fun activity with other kids.

Girls, on average, spend less time gaming. Their choices of genre are also often different. Cosette has no interest in role-playing games, but enjoys occasional games involving virtual animals:

> I do sometimes play games, but I'm not very involved. I play games that are easy to leave, like BeastKeeper (a fantasy pet breeding game where you can also build things) or Flight Rising (a game about breeding and raising dragons). I check in on the animals and my messages from others in the community. It's a relaxing game that's not very

> complicated. I took a break for six months and when I came back I wasn't caught up, but everyone was very nice to me.

Cosette had only negative things to say about the very popular MMOG *World of Warcraft*:

> I never got into it. I didn't want to pay for it and it's too complicated and too time-consuming. You spend the entire time fighting things. And if you're a new player, they're not very nice to you.

Some Developers are Trying to Build Healthier Games

Some developers are striving to create exciting games that are also meaningful and teach life lessons. Independent video game designer Jason Rohrer told an interviewer he is "trying to figure out how I can sort of check more commercial boxes in terms of making a game that would appeal to more people, while still feeling like it's something I'm really proud making. Something that touches on deep issues." He says the current market values visual presentation over interactive, thought-provoking stories. He says he is tired of seeing what he calls repetitive, mind-numbing video games.

The 37-year-old father of three also wants players to get more out of the time they spend playing. He says that the amount of meaning a gamer gets out of a certain period of time playing should be more concentrated. He views the big, long games as "meant to chew up your entire week."

When asked what recommendations he'd have for parents of gaming addicts, he suggested shifting away from never-ending games to those that have an endpoint, and are dense with meaningful content. He suggested games such as Fez, Braid, World of Goo, Antichamber, and Papers Please. Most of these games are puzzles that require manipulation of objects in space and inventive, original thinking. Independent designers who put up their own savings to create their work generally make them. They aren't generally bringing in the big bucks, and some of their work is actually a critique of contemporary trends in gaming.

Most of these games have clear end points, and are laden with challenges that require deep thought by the player versus mindless repetition or pure luck. They lend themselves to more discrete, shorter periods of play and more creative thinking.

Recreational versus Compulsive Gaming

We're not against recreational gaming. Recreational use doesn't disrupt usual routines, school, work, or relationships. This type of gaming is freely chosen and helps a person relax and return to their usual tasks refreshed and with more focus.

In comparison, compulsive gaming always negatively impacts other areas of life. Real-life socializing pales in comparison to virtual reality. Family relationships suffer. Former goals are abandoned or given so little attention that they have no chance of being met. Time spent on screen-based media has repeatedly been shown (for all youth) to reduce time reading, doing homework, and being with friends and family.

There are also dangerous physical consequences. Compulsive playing can cause headaches from eyestrain and sensory overload. Backaches that turn into chronic back problems are common from being seated in the same position for so long. Carpal tunnel syndrome can result from overuse of a mouse or game controller. Compulsive gamers are sleep deprived, and stay up all night so often that they reverse their sleep cycle. Diet suffers, because compulsive gamers either grab whatever food interferes the least with their game (junk food and sodas), or they skip meals entirely. Their room may be littered with dishes, junk food wrappers, and food itself.

Personal hygiene deteriorates. They may neglect basic hygiene like showers and keeping their hair clean. They may have a vitamin D deficiency due to being indoors so much. Their muscle tone may have atrophied.

Gaming Guidelines from The American Academy of Pediatrics and Others

The American Academy of Pediatrics recommends *zero* screen time for kids under age two, and no more than one to two hours of total entertainment screen time for older kids and teens. They advise keeping both televisions and Internet-connected devices out of the child's bedroom. They counsel parents to monitor what media their children are using, including all websites visited. They encourage parents to establish a family home use plan for all media, and as part of that plan to enforce mealtime and bedtime "curfews" for media devices.

Zero to Three, a national non-profit organization, offers research-based guidelines for screen use in children under three. They recognize that our world is now one of technology and that "screens are everywhere." With that in mind, they have some good advice for parents that would apply well to autistic children. They suggest participating with your child in any screen experience and making it a language-rich, interactive activity. They suggest asking questions and talking about what is on the screen, so that you expand your child's learning. They also suggest helping your child make a connection between what they see on the screen and the real world.

A way to do this is to play games using objects similar to what was on the screen, or to make up and act out pretend stories using whatever animals or objects were on the screen. They advise pointing out and labeling objects in real life that were seen on the screen.

They suggest that content should be chosen very carefully and should reflect your child's experiences in the real world, be organized around everyday themes, and depict positive interactions between people. They advise against fast-paced programs that don't allow your child to plan and organize information to reach a goal. Finally, they recommend avoiding media before bedtime, not snacking or eating meals while using media, and keeping it out of your child's bedroom.

Other researchers also stress how parents need to monitor the quality of what their children are accessing. Content should be high quality so that youth are learning something valuable. Otherwise, they should be outside getting exercise, or reading or doing hobbies, and using their imagination in free play.

How Gaming Is Designed to Work Like a Drug

Unrestricted gaming easily turns into compulsive or addictive gaming in kids on the spectrum. (We'll explain in detail why they are super-vulnerable later in this chapter.) Once addicted, they are preoccupied with gaming even when they're not actual playing. It becomes their special (but toxic) interest. They make excuses or lie to spend time online, and misrepresent how much time is consumed there.

Compulsive gaming turns them into a different kid. Other important activities or goals are neglected. They become detached and apathetic. If you express concern about their gaming they get defensive and angry. Compulsive gamers may buy games or accessories they can't afford, even stealing to make more purchases.

The manufacturers of online games intentionally design them to hook players. They precisely time and strategically place rewards into the game to maximize hitting the dopamine receptors in your kid's brain. Biologically, gaming works like any other addicting drug. Role-playing games in particular have become known as the crack cocaine of the gaming world. With so many rewards and a carefully engineered reinforcement schedule intentionally built into their design, these games create an experience that your child doesn't get anywhere else.

Instead of being bullied, ignored, or outcast, now your child has the opportunity to be a highly respected, valued person, even if it is in the form of their avatar. Imagine how good that feels. Patrick spoke bluntly about some of the reasons gaming was attractive.

> I like role-playing games and have an attraction to a white knight character. From a psychological perspective, I feel helpless about injustice in the world, so by playing the white knight I can punish wrongdoers. It's probably connected to being bullied. They are evil-doers in my head. I'd play every evening after school. I really got attached to role-playing games.

Game developers make extra rewards and challenges kick in as your child improves his skills and starts advancing to higher levels. The game is programmed *to respond to your child*. The more he advances, the more complex the game becomes. This progressively sucks your kid into the game and activates more dopamine. This schedule of frustration, followed by longing, the euphoric rush of achievement, and then the crash of meeting another preprogrammed game obstacle produces intense cravings.

Your child can increasingly build rankings, status, points, and goodies— as long as they don't stop playing. They can't stop playing, both because of the powerful rush, and because other players get ahead of them anytime they stop. That's another reason they hate leaving a game. Marina has had periods of time when she found it very difficult to break away from a game.

During summer breaks when I had nothing else to do, I often got obsessed with video games. I would play until I got sick. Usually the nausea stops me, but not always. If not, my husband will pull the plug and make me take a break and eat something.

Gaming Is Especially Dangerous to the Autistic Brain

It's easy to attribute excessive gaming to laziness, dullness, or a character flaw. But for many autistic youth, gaming represents a drug-like solution to multiple challenges inherent in their biological wiring. Children with ASD participate in screen-based activities (including television, video, and computer games) *more often than any other leisure activity* on both weekdays and weekends. Once autistic kids get into recreational gaming, they are more likely to turn into compulsive gamers than their NT peers.

A recent study looked at the relationship between gaming and problem behaviors in 169 boys aged 8 – 18 who had a diagnosis of autism. They measured average hours of gaming per day, type of games preferred (genres), play patterns, and behavior. They found compulsive gaming was associated with *both* attention problems and oppositional behavior. The greatest levels of oppositional behavior were found in boys who liked *role-playing games*, the favorite game genre of autistic kids. This held true no matter what age or how many hours the boy spent on the role-playing games.

Jaime makes a good point when he recognized how his focus on games was similar to his autistic patterns in general.

Gaming was more of a problem in my personal life, when I would home in on the game and ignore the outside world. From all I've read about those of us on the spectrum that is the norm; we have the tendency to hyper focus onto whatever's holding our attention at the moment, and so it was for me with games.

Using Electronics to Avoid Meltdowns Isn't Worth It

Unfortunately, parents of autistic kids have often been told it's really important that their kids are proficient on the computer. Too many autistic kids were introduced to computers and gaming way too early. Many parents were happy to find something that interested their toddler and reduced meltdowns. Technology often was the quickest solution. Lots of three-year-old kids regularly play with an iPad now instead of another three-year-old.

Patrick explained the appeal for him.

> For me, gaming was escapism. I played Mario since I was a toddler and then got serious on my eighth birthday when I got Nintendo 64. Those games were far more in depth and sucked me in more.

Parents of autistic kids report more problematic electronics use than parents of NT kids. Their children started playing video games and using electronic devices and the Internet at an earlier age than NT kids. The only online area that ASD kids got involved with at a later age than NT kids was social media, such as Facebook, Flickr, and Twitter.

This is dangerous, because *even at low or moderate levels of use, screen time probably has more pronounced effects on an autistic child*. The ASD brain is wired to love computer games because both are programmed similarly. Games are repetitive and inflexible, patterns autistic brains prefer. Autistic children exposed to computer games are at high risk for developing a preference for interacting with computers over people. When parents hand their toddlers screens, they may think it's a mindless distraction, but they are intensifying the rigid, restrictive tendencies of autistic brain wiring. Every time our kids play, they are strengthening inflexible ways of thinking.

Dr. Theodore Henderson is a child psychiatrist who specializes in ASD youth. He is really concerned about the addictive nature of video games. He told us that it is a true addiction. The best approach, in his opinion, is to prevent problems by limiting video game time to one or two hours a day. For older kids who are severely addicted, he recommends slowly reducing the time playing video games. He has had success with filling the teenagers' time up with hands-on activities such as car repairs. One severely addicted teenager had to be sent to a residential facility and all video games were removed. It took six months to gradually get the teenager to do other activities.

Your Child's Brain Changes Are Shaped by Experience

Our kids' brains actually change depending on what they are exposed to. All of our brains are "plastic." They change both how they function and how they're actually wired in response to how they are used. There's an old saying in neurology: "what fires together, wires together." When gamers incessantly use the same brain pathways, those pathways grow while others atrophy.

We know this happens any time brains devote tremendous amounts of time to a repetitive activity. MRI scans of London taxi drivers show obvious changes in both the function and actual structure of their brains in the area of spatial navigation. Scans of expert violinists show the part of the brain devoted to controlling their left fingers has changed and grown over the years. Scans of gamers look different than non-gamers'; they look like the brains of drug addicts. Their prefrontal cortex areas show impaired functioning. This part of the brain helps your kid make decisions, and stay motivated, flexible, and organized. Gamers do worse on tests involving memory and making decisions.

Gaming even shrinks the brain. Scans actually show less gray matter in gamers' brains than in non-gamers'. The more shrinkage, the more errors compulsive gamers made on the memory and decision making tests.

Autistic Brains Don't Have Central Heating

Here's a very simplified analogy to illustrate how the autistic brain works and how gaming impacts it. In a brain with typical autistic wiring, some parts work super efficiently while others are either sluggish or "offline." That's because the wiring is different from a neurotypical brain. Neural circuits are more specialized, producing uneven skill sets. This type of wiring results in a person's strengths and weaknesses both being magnified.

Let's assume you have central heating in your home. You can walk from one room to another and you don't experience big temperature changes. The central mechanism of your heater directs airflow so that it reaches all the rooms.

The autistic brain is like a house that has separate room heaters, and they work at different levels of efficiency. Some rooms are really hot, while others are a little warm, and others have no heater. Our kids on the spectrum have some rooms in their brains that put out tons of heat, and our job is to help them find a way to use that energy wisely. We also want them to find ways to get at least some warmth going in other, neglected rooms.

When our kids play certain video games, it's as though their brain wiring powers up the room heater with the most capacity to its highest setting. That room catches fire. The more they play the hotter it gets, and the colder the other rooms become.

In other words, the more the autistic brain is exposed to gaming and computer-based technology, the more it reacts with repetitive, inflexible thinking, communicating, and behaving. The prolonged hyper-focusing in compulsive gaming fortifies an already rigid, under-connected network. Their heating system (their brain's neural network) is not centralized and it doesn't spread its energy out. This is a problem in the neurotypical world, which demands flexibility in thinking and interacting, and the ability to use many parts of our brain. Some video games put our kids at even greater disadvantage.

Jaime, 35, commented on how hyper-focused he can get while gaming.

> It does sometimes become a problem with my partner, as she notices I get too zoned into the game. It's not that I play excessively, but that once in a game, I cannot easily leave its grasp on my attention.

Jaime is a good example of how fixated his brain becomes while playing even though he is not addicted to gaming. Fortunately, his parents prohibited him from playing video games during weekdays or after school, restricting him to weekends. With the laser focus that overtakes him when he does play, it's easy to imagine that he could have become a compulsive player without their limits. (He substituted reading during the week, for which he is grateful.)

Christopher Mulligan, a therapist who works with high functioning autistic teens and young adults, is highly troubled by gaming. He found that 90% of his clients (he's worked with over 500 in the past 12 years, doing groups, therapy, and consultation) grew up playing video games. He also found that 97% of them 18 and over are unemployed, and 99% are underemployed. He asks, "What's the biggest change in the world in the past decade? Computer technology is everywhere now and everyone is on it throughout the day. It is the biggest interest by far of the kids in my groups. They are way less interested in friendship. I have never seen a kid go through the process of courtship or dating that resulted in a long-term committed relationship. The long-term committed relationships they have are with their games."

Could Rates of Autism Be Influenced by Technology Use? One Therapist's Theory

Christopher believes that the dramatic rise in rates of autism in the past decade may be linked to the technology revolution. Kids born before smart phones and video games, even if they had highly compartmentalized brain wiring typical of autism, were just "geeks" who grew up and got jobs that required specialized knowledge or repetitive behaviors. But they also had other interests, relationships, and passable social skills. They would not have met the diagnostic criteria for autism, even high functioning or Asperger's.

But exposed to computers from an early age, the specialized brains of those kids may have "tipped" into diagnosable autism. He's not saying this had anything to do with kids born on the more severe end of the spectrum. He's talking about kids on the high functioning end of the autism spectrum, those who used to be diagnosed with Asperger's Disorder. (This term was eliminated in 2013 and incorporated into the new term Autism Spectrum Disorder, or ASD.)

His thinking makes sense to us. We are not ruling out biological factors as causes of the increased rate of autism. But we also think it is worth examining the chronology of the rate increase, and comparing that to when video games entered our lives. In 2002 the Centers for Disease Control (CDC) said 1 in 150 kids met diagnostic criteria for some type of autism. By 2010 the rate was 1 in 68. (No data is available past that year yet.) The original Xbox came out in 2001. Sony's Play-Station 2 came out in 2000. In the early 2000s a rash of massive multiplayer games came out.

Most kids on the high end of the autism spectrum don't get diagnosed until around 9 or 10 years old. What if kids born with highly specialized brain circuitry in the early 2000s were given computers to play with and got heavily into gaming? By about fourth grade their thinking might have become even more rigid and their flexible, creative thinking may have atrophied. Their social skills and interest in other hobbies may have declined. Teachers, parents, and therapists might start to be concerned about these kids and refer them for evaluation and help. By this point, it's possible their thinking patterns and behaviors looked like Asperger's or high functioning autism.

Christopher Mulligan thinks this is feasible.

> One thing is for certain. Three decades ago NO child was living inside their homes – isolated from peers and community, sitting in front of a computer scrolling through facts or images, playing video games, looping through YouTube videos, or watching a scene in a DVD for hours on end. If one were to sit down and design a form of environmental stimulation that would be toxic or damaging to the ASD brain by virtue of exacerbating the core neurological deficits, that stimulation is 21st century technology.

The Disappearance of Vocational Prep Classes in High School Has Hurt Our Kids

In addition to technology, there are also other cultural factors that might be associated with the rise in rates of autism. Schools used to have classes that exposed kids to skills needed in specific vocations. They included subjects such as home economics (which covered cooking, sewing, and managing a household, including a budget), woodworking, construction, welding, car repair, and plumbing. Not all schools had all of these classes, but if there was more than one school close enough to you, you might have been able to pick yours based on your future goals.

Budget cuts and cultural shifts emphasizing college attendance have changed this situation, and these classes are rarely available anymore. Our kids are not getting exposed to some of the trades that may work well for someone on the spectrum. For these youth, the skills they do have upon high school graduation don't translate into careers. College does not appeal to everyone, nor is it necessary for everyone.

When these young adults flounder, they may come to the attention of someone who is familiar with the typical signs of high functioning autism. If the young adult is still living at home, a concerned parent may read something about

Asperger's or HFA and wonder if their child fits this diagnosis. If their child is shy, awkward, a loner, and bright but not functioning at capacity, they may take that child to get evaluated.

In the old days, that young adult may already have moved out because they secured a job in a factory or company that used skills the person had already learned in a vocational class in high school. Or someone may have taken them on as an apprentice, which led to a steady job. Parents would not have been concerned if their kid was out on their own and financially making it, and it's unlikely they would have ever heard of the spectrum anyway in those days.

How Changes in Parenting Roles Impact Our Kids

Another non-biological factor that may be associated with more individuals meeting diagnostic criteria for the high end of the autism spectrum is the change in how we teach social skills. In the past 50 years we've seen parenting roles shift dramatically. Most parents used to intentionally teach their children life lessons from an authoritative perspective. They required specific behaviors at home, such as addressing other adults by title and greeting adults verbally or perhaps with a handshake.

Family roles were a given and stickers or charts weren't used as motivation. Punishment for not doing assigned tasks tended to be losing privileges or allowance (if given), or being grounded. While we're not advocating a return to the past, and we recognize great benefit in many parenting shifts, this one area has its drawbacks for autistic children. For kids on the spectrum, social skills and social manners need to be taught directly and concretely. These children will not naturally pick up how to appropriately interact with others on their own.

When autistic children grow up in families that do not explicitly teach social skills, they will likely increasingly lag behind peers. Similar to youth who enter young adulthood vocationally unprepared due to lack of exposure to trades, these kids are likely to attract someone's attention and concern these days, now that autism has received more public awareness. In the past, if they were taught social scripts, they may have stayed under the radar. The combination of children having been taught explicit social rules and autism not being in the community's general vocabulary, would have resulted in these kids never being evaluated or diagnosed.

One Doctor (and Former Game Addict) Says Your Child's Brain Becomes All Thumbs

Dr. Andrew Doan, author of "Hooked On Games," almost lost his marriage and medical career due to excessive gaming. He is passionate and opinionated about how games impact our children's brains. He believes games and autism simply do not mix and bluntly says, "If you are autistic, and game, you will become addicted." We won't go that far, but we do agree the risk is very high.

During a phone call, he explained that he believes what the brain practices is what the brain becomes. In a recent article he coauthored, he proposed an analogy to clarify how your child's central nervous system may develop when exposed to excessive gaming. "Observe your left hand. The thumb will represent the cortical areas associated with all the benefits of video gaming and use of technology: quick analytical skills, improved hand-eye-coordination, and perhaps improved reflexes. The index finger will represent the cortical areas associated with communication skills. The middle finger will represent behaviors associated with social bonding with family and friends. The ring finger will represent empathy, the capacity to recognize emotions of both self and others. Lastly, the little finger will represent the cortical areas associated with self-control.

"While these higher executive functions are biologically based, they will not fully develop without proper practice and feedback. Now fold your fingers into the palm of your hand. This represents what happens when your child has too much screen time. Their hand is now just a thumb. They become a young adult whose brain is all thumbs in their thinking: possessing quick analytical skills and quick reflexes, but not as developed in communication skills, having few bonds with people, exhibiting little empathy, and showing minimal self-control."

Gaming Deprives Your Child of Other Skills

Screen time is time not interacting with others in the real world. This deprives our kids of learning social skills, how to negotiate differences, and how to resolve problems. It also misses opportunities to expose our kids to lots of different kinds of people with lots of various interests. One of them may turn into a mentor and one of the interests may turn into a career.

Online games don't demand the skills that real relationships do. You can yell at the computer and it won't punish or desert you. You can even throw things or hit it (and lots of kids do). You can stomp away and no one questions or comes after you. As Dan, age 47, said, "Online social interactions are easier and safer in some ways because you can pull the plug at a moment's notice if you get overwhelmed." Since online relationships are anonymous, no one is accountable or on their best behavior. Comments by players are often brutal and very immature—just what you don't want your kid being exposed to. Instead of teaching empathy, disdain, cruelty, and hostility are modeled.

Yet even if your child engages in these inappropriate interactions, it's highly unlikely those in the online community will reject them. And that teaches them a lesson about life that's untrue. In the real world, people won't put up with that sort of immaturity or rudeness.

Games also teach your child to rely on external distractions to self-soothe. They don't get practice developing this important skill if they automatically turn on a game every time they are in a bad mood or stressed out.

Autistic Kids are Trying to Satisfy Unmet Needs

ASD gamers are usually fulfilling otherwise unmet needs. Even if your kid doesn't seem to care about other people, they probably do. Like all of us, they need validation and acknowledgement from others. They get a false sense of that through online games. They suddenly belong to a group and have an identity within a virtual community. That's very powerful to your child. Others players won't reject your child, because they want them (i.e., their avatar) to keep playing.

Children on the spectrum are also attracted to online gaming because a fantasy world is easier to manage than real life. It comes with a set of clear rules, structure, and repetition. The rules don't change, and they are even codified in thick books that many kids pore over. This environment is preferred to interacting with complex, confusing people. The real world is chaotic. Virtual reality is predictable.

Games Cause Heart Rates to Skyrocket and Moods to Plummet

Our kids don't actually relax when they are gaming. They are in a constant state of arousal they've acclimated to. They have no idea how high their heart rates go while gaming. ASD players also get intensely upset if they find a glitch in a game or a game character is given an action the player doesn't approve of. Debra had to re-direct therapy sessions when adolescent male clients came to their appointment highly agitated, having just quit playing a game, and wanting to obsessively talk about how stupid a game developer was.

Internet addiction is linked to chronic depression. The more addicted your child is, the more their mood plummets after only *15 minutes* of exposure to the Internet! This can create a vicious cycle—they go online, they rapidly feel worse, then they stay online longer trying to feel better. It's a self-fueling addiction.

The lonelier your child is, the more likely they are to engage in compulsive gaming. And the more they play, the lonelier they get. Low self-esteem and low social competence have been found to predict later pathological gaming.

Male gamers who play the most hours per week started playing at earlier ages and have more severe depression and social phobia, and stronger gaming addiction than those who play fewer hours. Female gamers play less, and start at a later age. But once they start, they develop even more severe depression, more somatic issues such as pain, and greater social phobia the longer they play.

Brain scans show that gamers identify more strongly emotionally with their avatar than with their biological self. These same gamers also had better memory for their avatars than for other people in their lives. This increased the more they played.

Compulsive Gaming Distances Your Kid From You & Others

Compulsive gamers often let real friendships languish to the point of extinction. This is dangerous. Real-life friends give real-life support. You go out in the world with them and they visit you. You try new activities with them and help each other out in practical ways like giving each other a ride. In real-life friendships you have to learn how to control your voice, face, and other actions in face-to-face conversations. A lack of real-world friends, especially at a young age, damages a person's ability to properly socialize.

Compulsive gaming changes children's relationships with parents and other adults. They begin to resent anything that stands in the way of being online. This includes having meals with the family. They want to eat in their room while gaming. They stay up half (or all) of the night playing, and their sleep cycle reverses. They may rarely see their parents or siblings anymore.

One Mother's Story: Gaming Can Be Deadly

Shawn Woolley had epilepsy as a child. But his seizures didn't stop him from clowning around or graduating from high school. He never had romantic relationships, but he had some friends, even though he didn't believe he was really liked or accepted. He wasn't athletic, but he was interested in art from an early age, and was good at it. But his life unraveled after high school, as he started spending pretty much all of his time playing the MMOG *EverQuest*, one of the most popular and profitable role-playing games ever.

His brother Tony, in an online video, said, "When he graduated from high school, I think he kinda found out it was a little tougher in the real world than in high school. Everything was going good in the game world and he liked that a lot better."

His family life deteriorated, and he and his mother frequently argued about gaming. He neglected all areas of his life except gaming and resented any attempts to engage him in real life. Liz, his mom, says she became the "bad person—he thought if I'd just leave him alone he'd be happy." He barely even managed to tear himself away from his game to attend his brother's wedding, and photos from that day clearly show him sullen. He objected to being taken away from *EverQuest*, and he left early to go back to playing, missing the entire reception.

Shawn Woolley before and after he got immersed in role-playing video games.

Even though Shawn got mad at anyone who criticized how much he was playing, he may have realized how out of control his gaming was. In gaming forums, *EverQuest* is actually referred to as "Ever Crack" (referring to the highly addicting qualities of the game). The term has even made it into the website www.urbandictionary.com.

Shawn began having grand mal seizures while playing, but even that didn't deter him. Finally there was a family confrontation and he was told there would be no more playing the game in the house. His mother removed the computer keyboard and hid the modem. Shawn trashed the house looking for it.

Under pressure, he agreed to get help and entered a residential county mental health program, where he was diagnosed with depression and schizoid personality disorder (he had been diagnosed with ADD earlier in life). It should be noted that in speaking with Shawn's mom by phone, she said Asperger's or autism was never mentioned and she didn't know much about these conditions.

Professionals unfamiliar with ASD often misattribute the social challenges of autism to schizoid personality. A personality disorder is defined as a pattern of behaviors and inner experience that deviates from the expectations of a person's culture and develops during adolescence or adulthood. This contrasts with ASDs, which are neurological differences present throughout life and include restricted interests. It's impossible to know if Shawn may have been on the spectrum, but he did show early, specialized interest in art and design, and we know that ⅓ of children with autism develop epilepsy. He also seemed to care deeply what others thought of him, while indifference to praise or criticism is on the list of diagnostic criteria for schizoid personality.

In any case, even the professionals didn't seem to "get" how important and risky Shawn's gaming addiction was. While in the county program, and on medication, he progressed and moved out into his own apartment, which was supported by his therapists. There's no indication that a treatment protocol for gaming addiction was used with Shawn.

Once in his own apartment, Shawn went right back to compulsive gaming. He worked long enough to buy a computer, and then didn't show up for his job. He disconnected his phone, wouldn't answer the door, and failed his counseling appointments. He played *EverQuest* constantly for two weeks.

On Thanksgiving Day, 2002, Shawn's mom decided to try yet again to reach him so that he might spend at least part of the holiday with his family. She went to his apartment and found his door unlocked, but the security chain in place. "I could smell something and I knew something was wrong. I went home and got a hammer and screwdriver and came back and cut the chain off."

Shawn's mother found her son sitting in front of his computer. *EverQuest* was playing in the background. Shawn had shot and killed himself in the middle of the game.

Liz tried to get Sony, the company that made *EverQuest*, to release data about her son's last gaming activities. They refused. She believes something happened while Shawn was playing that he couldn't handle. His most recent avatar's name was "ILuvYou," and her best guess is that his avatar had asked another avatar to marry him or enter a romantic relationship. "I don't think he could really distinguish between online fantasy life and real life at that point. He had no love life on earth. He was betrayed by the only world he cared about."

Liz has since started a support group for compulsive gamers and their families. We include information on it at the end of this chapter in the resource section.

How Game Developers Manipulate Role-Playing Gamers

Online games are very big business. Worldwide sales have gone up every year and are expected to top $112 *billion* in 2015. Companies who develop these games put extensive money and research into designing the most compelling games possible. There are scores of companies competing for your child's interest. They want your child to purchase the initial software and accessories, to become so involved in the game that they play frequently, and subsequently buy the continually marketed updates and sequels.

Martin Koppel, CEO of Fortumo, a company that game developers use to manage the systems whereby gamers make payments, stated, "Games with excellent content and quality will keep players coming back for thousands of game sessions, and it is a logical consequence that these games also make the biggest profit. Staying on top of the charts for a long time requires creating an addictive game which has just the right amount of monetization to not break game play."

In some ways, this is no different than the strategy of many businesses. To make money, most companies need repeat customers. The difference is that repeated use of some video games turns into compulsive use in some customers, and we're discovering that males with autistic brain wiring are at particular risk. The compulsive feeds on itself as their brains become more vulnerable over time. Other products, such as alcohol and cigarettes, that carry this type of risk are regulated and include warning labels. But we are just beginning to realize how powerful the newer MMOGs are and how much they impact our children's brains. We predict that as more and more families realize their sons are unable to stop gaming and get a real life, we'll start to wake up and see how pervasive and dangerous online gaming can be.

One Wake-Up Call Already Happening: Competitive Gamers' Use of Performance Enhancing Drugs Banned as of July 2015

Gaming is a big enough business to have spawned the term "eSports," and there are hugely attended international competitions held regularly. As this chapter was being written, the Electronic Sports League (ESL) just issued a press release announcing that one of the major gamers had admitted to using performance-enhancing drugs on a regular basis. As a result, the ESL will begin drug testing at all competitions.

One gaming researcher told us she had heard the term "digital doping" used to refer to players enhancing their avatars by purchasing extra powers to give them an advantage over competitors. Now it appears that competitive players may also be routinely doping themselves. In July 2015, a leading competitive gamer from the U.S., Kory Friesen, admitted to taking Adderall, a stimulant used to treat ADHD, at an ESL competition in Poland. He said his former teammates also use the stimulant (it contains amphetamine) so they can play for long periods of time and react more quickly. "We were all on Adderall. It was pretty obvious...tons of people do it ... like it's pretty obvious," Mr. Friesen said. His interviewer asked, "Everyone does Adderall ... right?" and Kory responded, "Yeah." "Just throwing that out there for the fans," the interviewer then said flippantly. "That's how you get good."

Developers Hire Psychologists to Maximize the Power of Games

It may surprise you to know that many (probably most, maybe all) gaming companies have psychologists on staff. They are hired for their knowledge of how to best manipulate gamers. One, Mike Ambinder, Ph.D., said his role is to apply knowledge and methodologies from psychology to game design, for example, by telling developers how to use reward/reinforcement ratios, how to foster action among players, and how to manipulate visual attention onscreen.

Dr. Ambinder, in a publicly posted PowerPoint presentation on his company's website, noted that researchers used to adjust game design by getting gamers' verbal feedback. He noted, though, that "People don't know why they do what they do." So instead of the traditional method of question and answer interviews with gamers, his presentation described in detail emerging technologies, or more "technical" approaches. These methods include collecting physiological measurements directly from your child, which were noted to have the advantages of being involuntary and objective because they couldn't be faked.

Dr. Ambinder has described how experiments using sensors collect gamers' physiological reactions while playing. Data on heart rate, eye movements, gestures, facial expressions, tone of voice, muscle contraction, skin electrical conductance, EEGs (noted to be expensive, and very intrusive!), and respiration rate have been studied. This information is being collected in order to shed light on your child's type of emotion and intensity of emotion while gaming. With that information, developers make adjustments to the game, and compare gamers' responses to see which design maximizes arousal, or as they'd term it, "enjoyment." We call it compulsion at best, addiction at worst.

Behind the Scenes at Gaming Conferences—One Woman's Discoveries

Regine Pfeiffer, a retired teacher from Germany, become interested in what was happening behind the scenes in game development when she was teaching computer skills at a grammar school over 10 years ago. She was in her mid-60s at the time. *World of Warcraft* had recently been released. She saw how compelling the game was, especially for her male students. After she started doing public presentations about the dangers of compulsive playing, she was cyber bullied and even received death threats. That was a decade ago, and she continues to write about gaming addiction, contributing a chapter to a book published in Germany in 2015: "Internet and computer addiction: A practical manual for therapists, educators and parents."

Regine said she decided to use her own funds to attend gaming industry conferences so she could hear what the developers were saying behind closed doors. "The people there did not mind my presence. My age makes me appear harmless, and even when I spoke up and said who I was and why I was attending, they were only amused." What she found out may surprise you.

She wrote that at a 2009 Virtual Goods Summit in San Francisco, one presenter, Chinese developer Zhan Ye, said, "Good monetization design is based on deep understanding of human psychology. In a sense, game designers are exploiting people's weaknesses … in a sense, F2P games are operated like casinos in Las Vegas." This PowerPoint file was still accessible online when this book went to press.

Regine wrote that in 2011 she attended another conference, the Social Goods Summit in Berlin, and was allowed to tape record Julian Hühnermann's presentation, "Monetization and Balancing in Browser Games." She stated that this presentation also used to be posted online, but has been removed. She said the speaker discussed "balancing," a concept in game design that means fine-tuning a game's rules so it's competitive with other games on the market. According to Regine, he elaborated on two types of balancing: "soft balancing," which works on the principle of fairness, and "hard balancing," which does not. Regine wrote that Mr. Hühnermann said hard balancing is where the greatest profits are made, and that he wouldn't let his own children play these types of games.

Your child may not be spending money upgrading their avatar or purchasing accessories. Players who spend tremendous amounts of money on games are known as "whales." It's the same exact term casinos use for the big spenders. These players (in both worlds) are not in the majority, but they bring in the most profit.

But independent game developer Jason Rohrer pointed out that this creates its own issue; "The less a gamer pays, the more they have to play to reach the same level as someone who pays. This may in fact increase their addiction, because they go through the reinforcement loop so many extra times (grinding their way up instead of paying to jump up immediately)."

What's a Parent to Do?

First, if you're not there yet, get out of denial. Call it what it is. If your child plays more than an hour or two of online games per day, it's probably compulsive by now, and they can't stop on their own. If they play most of the day, they have a serious addiction in our opinion, and it is robbing them of a better life. We're not trying to vilify technology or all video games (Debra loves playing online word games as a relaxing break, though Temple says if she started she knows she would become addicted). We realize technology isn't going anywhere—it's part of our life now and there's no turning back. But it absolutely does not have to dominate your child's life. We should be masters of our technology, not the other way around.

There may be some teens on the spectrum who can play several hours some days, but here's how you tell it's not a problem: they also are doing okay at their job, volunteer activities, or school; they interact appropriately with real people; they participate in family activities without resenting being away from their games; they don't talk incessantly about their games; and they have other offline interests they engage in regularly.

Get the Whole Family on Board

Your first step is to try to get the whole family on board. Parents united as a team have much more impact. If you are a mom reading this, and you think your husband is also a compulsive gamer, have that discussion first. Consider having it in front of a therapist so that your communication is calmer and more effective. If your child has a therapist who will see the whole family, call them and schedule an appointment for this discussion.

You can't expect your child to cut back on gaming if you're obsessed with screen activities yourself. If your life consists of watching TV and movies, constantly being on Facebook, or playing games on a device, then your actions speak louder than your words. Plus you're going to need that time for interacting with your child as you find replacement activities for their gaming (which we'll talk more about later).

Find out if your child's therapist is aware of the extent of their gaming. Surprisingly, many aren't. Your child isn't going to volunteer the information and unless the therapist is savvy about gaming, and asks very direct questions, your child will give vague or misleading answers about how much they game.

There are fairly standard strategies for breaking addictions, although treatment of compulsive gaming in autistic kids has barely been studied. The kids got way ahead of us on this. The two most important things you need to know are: (1) you have to be fully and consistently involved and on board, and (2) if a therapist or treatment facility is involved they should ideally be familiar with both autism and treating compulsions. Unfortunately, at this point, it's next to impossible to find these resources in most communities. We are still in denial about how big this problem is.

Even the Mental Health Profession Has Not Caught Up Yet

Dr. Kimberly Young, who pioneered awareness of Internet addiction over 20 years ago, compares it to smoking. "We had plenty of evidence that smoking was addicting and even deadly. But no one wanted to admit it because so many people smoked and enjoyed it, and it was a huge and lucrative industry. It took many years of destroyed lives before we woke up and admitted the danger. Internet addiction is now in the same position. Even the mental health profession has swept it under the rug."

Dr. Young acknowledged that she was unfamiliar with the research on gaming addiction and autism. The connection immediately made sense to her, though, and during our conversation she decided to include a chapter specifically on Internet addiction and autism in her upcoming book on treatment for children and teens.

How to Create Your Own Intervention

Since few therapists are familiar with both autism and Internet addiction, for now it falls to parents to take the lead. We are going to outline what you must consider in helping your child break their addiction, and we are going to walk you through steps to take. Give this section to your child's therapist, if they have one, and hopefully you can all work together. But if there is no therapist in the picture, don't let that stop you. You can be a powerful influence on your child, and they desperately need you to intervene.

Your goal is to stop your child's compulsive gaming. But it's *equally* important that you help rebuild the parts of your child's life that have been lost over time. These include their confidence, healthy daily habits, relationships, and plans for the future.

Interestingly, adult gamers on the spectrum acknowledge that the games are time sucks and can be addicting. They also recognize that they are just filling time. In one study, they told the researchers games help "kill time," or "pass a boring day," and can be a good "time waster." They realize they are unproductive.

Emotionally, your child is probably in a crappy place. No matter what they might say, they know others their age are moving on, not sitting in their bedroom playing video games. They are discouraged at best and may be clinically depressed. If they have social phobias, they've probably gotten more entrenched, at least when it comes to real, live people. They usually feel a level of shame, mixed with resentment that the world won't leave them alone. While games periodically reward your child with rushes of dopamine, they routinely frustrate your child too. As a result, your teen may have developed a hair-trigger temper and become more cynical.

Step # 1 – Know Your Child's Patterns and Triggers

We'll discuss how to set restrictions in the next section. Before you get to that, you need to know how much your child is actually online. Make a simple chart—it doesn't have to be fancy. You will use it to monitor change and know when you've reached goals. If your child is in therapy, they can make one with their therapist.

The chart should include five things. First, the date and time your child goes online. Second, what they were doing right before they went online. You need to know this because you want to discover any patterns or "triggers" of the behavior. Third, write down exactly what the child did while on the computer. Were they on a chat room, a particular game, an Internet site, randomly surfing? Fourth, precisely how long they stayed online.

The last thing you write down is all the results of that episode of online activity. This part of the chart could include things like "missed dinner," didn't go to sleep until midnight," "argued with his brother about computer use," "was more irritable afterwards," "yelled at the computer." Write down everything that is negative. Have your child sign their name each day on the chart. That means they read it and saw what an outsider saw.

Keep the chart going even after your child is no longer gaming compulsively. However long it takes, don't give up on the chart. Its purpose is to figure out their baseline use, but also to visibly show their progress.

Step # 2 – Putting Restrictions in Place

Tell your child you are going to do this after two weeks of monitoring their use. Tell them you're waiting because you both need to know the extent of the problem. Occasionally this will cause a child to cut back (temporarily) to "show you" they don't have a problem, but few of them can control their gaming enough to do this.

Your child lives in a world where they're going to be around computers and other screen media the rest of their lives. They may even spend a fair amount of time on them as part of their work. Compulsive gaming is not like alcoholism—you can't abstain 100% in today's world. It's more like someone with a food addiction; they still need to eat, but they have to figure out a healthy diet and a balanced life.

You must decide how much time to allow your child to be online, and what activities are prohibited. For instance, you may allow two hours per day of total screen time, but only one hour of it can be as part of a multiplayer role-playing game. Maybe the other hour can be in chat rooms or playing educational games. We think the American Academy of Pediatrics guidelines of one to two hours per day make sense. Gaming, or other non-work or non-school related screen activities, should be a minor part of a person's life. They should be reserved for the time remaining after taking care of responsibilities like school, homework, volunteering, going to work, helping out at home, daily hygiene, adequate sleep, sit-down meals, activities that involve movement and getting outside, face-to-face interactions, engaging with family members, reading, and other hobbies. Explain to your child that it's not so much a matter of time, but a matter of priorities.

Scott, 28, went through periods of more or less time spent gaming, and a big part of it had to do with whether his parents were monitoring him.

> I turned to video games to escape, but my parents had rules. I got home at 3:00 and was allowed to play for one hour from 4:00 until 5:00. Then I had to shut down the game and do two hours of homework. Schedule and routine were very important in our house. But there was a time period when my parents were preoccupied, and I starting gaming later at night, sometimes until 1:00 a.m. I was useless the next day at school. And there were weekends I'd play eight hours straight. My parents would scold me but we didn't have the same kind of structured rules on weekends, so I wouldn't listen.

Write down your rules for time allowed online. Use an alarm or egg timer to signal the end of allowed activity. Consider using filtering software to block access to prohibited sites. You can find a list of reputable companies on www.Internet-safety101.org, a site that's been around over 20 years and is sponsored by both non-profits and well-known corporations.

Most kids with autism have a strong sense of justice and fairness, and you should bring up the injustice of their wasting too much time gaming. Does your child think it is morally right for them to spend most of their time entertaining themselves instead of contributing to the family and the world? If they are old enough to hold a job, and making no effort to get one, do they think it is fair to be a financial parasite on their parents?

Those may sound like harsh words. Yet in counseling sessions Debra found that discussed in a matter-of-fact way, the logic of these questions made sense to autistic youth, who generally are great kids who want to do what is right. Many ASD teens are quite rigid in their judgments of how people should live honest, moral lives. They need someone to point out to them that living as a reclusive gamer has moral implications that contradict these strong beliefs.

Get the Computer Out of Their Bedroom

Remove the child's computer from their bedroom. Get creative. If you can't find room for it anywhere else, put it in the laundry room if necessary. Wherever it is, the door to that room must stay open.

The biggest predictor of oppositional behavior in ASD male gamers is whether they play in their bedroom or in a shared family space. The second biggest predictor is lack of parental restriction. This implies that many parents have it backwards—they fear conflict if they place restrictions on their sons, but if they don't, *that's* when oppositional behavior increases.

Compulsive gamers have become bedroom hermits. One anonymous 20-year-old put it this way:

> I lived in my bedroom. We had a nice, big house, but I could lock my door and be completely isolated from the real world. All the gamers did it. We were always in our bedroom. It was a completely private fantasy world. Everybody knew not to come knocking on my bedroom door.

What If My Child Refuses to Cooperate?

Expect tremendous resistance. Realize that the intensity of your child's defiance is a direct reflection of how addicted they are and how vital it is for you to intervene. You've probably made empty threats about "taking away" their computer before and didn't do it, or gave it back even though nothing changed. Your child is unlikely to take you seriously, and you can't blame them. You may have been actively enabling them for a long time. Some moms have even gotten into the habit of letting their kids eat meals while gaming. That has to stop immediately.

Tell your child that you realize they don't believe this time is going to be any different, and you can't blame them for that. But tell them *it is definitely going to be different this time* and that many eyes are upon them. Let them know that their therapist (if they have one) is going to be a big part of this. If they don't have a therapist, let them know that all family members are on board (including any close extended family like cousins, grandparents, or aunts or uncles they look up to) in supporting this.

Make sure you say that the whole idea is that they deserve a full life, not one shut up in their bedroom wasting time on games, and that everyone wants to see them succeed. Do not—no matter how frustrated you are—approach this as a punishment or in a shaming manner. Your child is going to need a lot of positive support and encouragement to get through this.

100% Unsupervised Total Withdrawal Not Advised

Start by restricting your child's gaming time, not eliminating it totally. First, you have to build replacement activities to fill your child's days. Later, some kids will find a way to game in a healthy manner. Others will need to stay away completely. It's too early to know that yet.

For now, allow your child one or two hours of screen time per day *after* other responsibilities are handled. If your child cannot or will not respect those limits, remove all computers from the premises (not just their bedroom) or lock them away where only you can get to them. Remove computer cables when you're not home. Change your child's password. Refuse to drive your child anywhere else they can play (like someone's house, an Internet café, or an arcade). If they want to have a friend over, monitor them closely, with doors always open, so you know they're not gaming on the friend's phone or other device.

Your child may have actual physical withdrawal, with headaches and anxiety. Ask them directly if they are experiencing this. Tell them it is a result of their brain adjusting, and is important data proving that their excessive gaming was changing their brain. These symptoms will likely pass within a day or two.

Let your child know what the consequences will be if they violate your restrictions. Some kids have broken down locked doors, cut through locks, or even stolen computers to feed their compulsion. We recommend you let them know you will call the police if they destroy property, threaten you, threaten to harm themselves, or do anything illegal. Then do it.

Most kids will throw a fit, but not go to these extremes. Ignore meltdowns that aren't safety risks and walk away from yelling. Never get sucked into a debate. Instead, state firmly, "This is not open to discussion because it is a severe problem and we care too much to ignore it anymore."

Another option is to send them away to a relative who is willing to strictly monitor them. There are a few wilderness camps for Internet addiction, but we haven't found any familiar with ASD. Throwing a kid with autism into a rough wilderness program with NT kids may do more harm than good. We only found one residential treatment program familiar with autistic youth, and it only takes five kids at a time for now. We'll list and describe it in the resource section at the end of this chapter.

We desperately need more out-of-home programs. This would eliminate parents giving in; there would be family meetings, and your child would be fully evaluated and treated for other issues like depression and anxiety. Residential programs for addiction include lots of support, skill building, and relapse prevention techniques. If you find a program for gamers on the spectrum, please let us know about it so we can spread the word.

Be Your Child's Coach or Find Them One

Since intensive programs are not yet widely available, you're either going to be your child's coach or you're going to work with a therapist or coach to help your child. A coach can be someone with an actual certificate, or simply someone who is familiar with autism or your child. A coach doesn't have to cost money. You may be able to find a high school or college student by posting a flyer at local schools or Starbucks. Maybe a retired teacher or neighbor can help. The most important thing is to teach them basic concepts and that your child gets along fairly well with them. You know your kid—match them accordingly.

You are with your child every day. Even if you do have a therapist, they probably only see your child once a week. That is not enough to break an addiction unless there is intensive support provided by you or someone else during the week. We wish it were different, but that's not what experience tells us.

We talked about cognitive behavioral therapy (CBT) earlier in the chapter on depression and anxiety. CBT is also routinely used for addiction problems and

Dr. Young, who was quoted a few pages back, has developed a modified version specifically for Internet addiction (CBT-IA). She doesn't work with autism, but her approach can be tweaked to take into consideration the special needs of those on the spectrum.

Dr. Young's approach, like most addiction treatment models, repeatedly confronts irrational or distorted beliefs that trigger or reinforce the addictive behavior. The main one for ASD kids who game compulsively is "I'm not hurting anybody, what's the big deal?" In other words, they're in denial. This has to be dealt with first.

Use Logic and a List to Show Your Child How Gaming is Harmful

Appealing to logic works better with ASD kids than appealing to emotion. Sit down with your child and together make a list of all the ways their gaming hurts others, and who it specifically hurts. Begin the sentence with these words: "My gaming hurts _____ by _____ ." Rewrite and repeat this sentence over and over the same exact way. This rhythm of the sentence is repetitive, which the autistic brain responds to.

Here are some examples: "My gaming hurts Mom because I don't greet her when she gets home from work." "My gaming hurts Dad because we don't take walks anymore." "My gaming hurts Mom and Dad because I am gaming instead of looking for a job, and they are struggling financially and Dad has to work extra hours and is exhausted." "My gaming hurts my grandmother because I don't visit her anymore even when she is sick."

Dan, 47, limited and changed his gaming once he realized how it was hurting his wife.

> I have always played video games. It became a problem when I got married and my wife wanted more attention than I gave my online gaming. I have since mostly quit that style of game. Now I play games with more versatile options and timing. That way I don't make commitments to my wife that I don't end up keeping. I simply had to make a choice when I realized my wife needed more attention. I was making her feel bad and that made the games no longer fun for me. I get those needs met now by playing games with friends in real life on occasion, and

playing video games when I'm alone. I also make concrete plans with my wife now, rather than leaving those interactions always tentative. That has helped us both feel more secure in the relationship.

List #2: Show Your Child How Gaming Contradicts Their Moral Beliefs

Now make another list. This one shows how gaming contradicts the lifestyle your child thinks is morally right. Most ASD youth have high moral standards and rigid rules of what is right and wrong. They tend to disdain those who take advantage of others. They have been bullied, mistreated, and taken advantage of in the past, and often have lingering anger about it. Show them that they themselves are being hypocrites by spending the majority of their time gaming, because this is a way of being a bully to their family by mooching and ignoring them. *Most ASD youth hate hypocrites.* They will find it difficult to dispute your logic when you show them specifically how they are neglecting reasonable responsibilities and being irresponsible.

Here are some examples: "I do not make an equal contribution to household chores," "I do not join the family for dinner because I put my gaming before my family," and "I game instead of getting a job because I have chosen to have others pay my way in this world."

It is very important that you reinforce to your child that you love him and you are simply pointing out evidence based on behavior. You want your child to know that you believe he is basically a good person, so praise his good qualities during these conversations. Point out the contradictions between his beliefs and his behavior. Tell him that this is what happens when someone becomes addicted to something—the addiction takes control and ignores morality. Your ASD child will likely hate hearing this because spectrum kids do not like being out of control. You are intentionally creating as much internal conflict as possible in order to begin breaking your child's denial.

Get Inside Your Kid's Head

You must be genuinely curious about your child's favorite game. Have them walk you through it. They are more likely to respect your opinion if you have some knowledge of their world. Find out if they use an avatar, and how they chose and designed the character. What skills did they give the avatar? What do they admire about the character? What avatars don't they like and why? This information is helpful because it gives you insight into what your child values. Those values are going to guide you in finding replacement activities to fill the time they previously spent gaming.

Find out what they like and dislike about gaming in general and about their favorite game in particular. Ask what it provides them. They'll likely just give you a vague answer at first: "It's fun," or "It's challenging," but keep pushing. Openly talk to your child about why gaming can be especially compelling for those on the autism spectrum. Go back to the beginning of this chapter and share the information about how the developers design games to hook them. Talk about how the autistic brain seems particularly vulnerable to gaming. Discuss how they are escaping and stalling their development.

Ask them if perhaps they don't want to grow up. You may be surprised to hear them admit that it terrifies them. This is a conversation you need to have. Remember that part of this battle is setting limits, but it's also about building up your child so they can resist this compelling escape, feel better about themselves, and get a real life.

Gamers know that most of their peers have moved on past recreational gaming into real lives, with friends, activities, and college or a job. They may fear they've wasted so much time that they'll never catch up. So they give up. Tell them it is never too late and you are there to help. Don't tell them to "get a real life." *To them, this is their life and it's real.* Let them know there are thousands of people in the world who have learned to manage gaming and get on with life. They are not alone.

Many compulsive gamers are suffering from depression. Schedule an evaluation—they may need an antidepressant. There is some new research showing that the antidepressant Wellbutrin (bupropion), given in sustained release form, decreases cravings for video games. In one small study, 150 mg/day was given for one week, and then was increased to 300 mg/day for five more weeks. At the end of the six weeks, cravings reduced by about 24%, total playing time reduced by 35%, and scores in an Internet addiction scale decreased 15%. While this was a small study, these are fairly impressive numbers given that the gamers were not given any other psychological treatment.

What Will Replace Gaming?

Daniel, 25, realizes the importance of having a replacement for excess computer time.

> I recently started to keep myself from watching so much anime and playing Minecraft until at least I do something productive. It helps me finish my chores. This was my own idea. It seems like a pretty simple idea, but the problem is if you could just arbitrarily keep yourself from doing something, you'd do it in the first place. You will fill your time with it if there's nothing else to do. I could just replace it with something else, but it has to be something better, not just any replacement.

Daniel is right. We can't expect our children to give up gaming if they have nothing to replace it with. As soon as we restrict their use, and while we are exploring their distorted, negative beliefs about themselves, we also have to get very actively involved in creating new activities and interests. You can't tear down a barn until you've built a new one or you will have animals running wild, getting lost, and getting hurt. It's the same for your child.

The next chapter in this book tells you how to teach vital life skills to your teen. An adult needs proficiency in tasks necessary to live independently (or even semi-independently in the case of less able individuals). For most compulsive gamers, they are way behind on these skills. Learning and practicing these skills, plus exploring new interests, will fill the hours previously wasted online.

Many high functioning spectrum teens have no idea what to do for a living, even though they have the intelligence and capability to work. Too many parents are assuming their child should go on disability because either (1) the child hasn't yet developed work skills, or (2) the parent feels overwhelmed and this seems like the easy way to go. There are some on the autism spectrum who legitimately require government financial aid. We support that. But higher functioning folks on the spectrum, once they discover their strengths and interests and match them with a vocation, are capable of being good, reliable, valued employees.

In addition to learning skills, your child needs to have fun. For some autistic teens, this is primarily interwoven with working or volunteering. Those arenas may provide adequate social contact, and the rest of their day can be spent with the typical tasks of an independent adult, like shopping, running errands, cooking, keeping up their living space, and perhaps tending to a garden or pet. If that leaves an hour or two for watching a movie or being on the computer, that's fine. It's balanced.

Patrick no longer spends as much time playing video games. This changed after he began volunteering and as he became involved in his voice-over training.

> I still play games, but it's more like I pop in to "do my dailys"—I have a daily goal to get a certain number of points. But we moved my computer out of my room when I needed to construct a recording studio there for my voice-over auditions. And when I got my volunteer job I had to get up in the morning, so I couldn't stay up all night playing. Plus now I use the computer for other things, like applying for jobs, submitting examples of my voice work, and just using Google search to learn about new things.

Find Better Things for Your Kid to Do

Your child does not have to have as many outside activities as NT youth. That may overload them and serve no purpose. But many of our youth don't know what they like because they never attempted much. Get them out of the house to see if they enjoy activities they've never tried or still like ones they used to do when they were younger. The list of possibilities is long. Some ideas are walking, hiking, kite flying, geocaching (using GPS to hide and find things), swimming, kayaking, collecting things from nature (feathers, shells, etc.), bird watching, playing catch, gardening, flying model airplanes, laser tag, biking, exploring caves, clay pigeon or skeet shooting, outdoor music concerts, taking a drive, croquet, dog walking, horse riding, landscape painting, photography, open air theatre, remote control cars or drones, Frisbee, fishing, rafting, skateboarding, or checking out local parks.

Other ideas include visiting a museum (of art, science, technology, history, or obscure items), going to the library (which often has a variety of activities offered), checking out special interest clubs (check your community paper, newsletter, website, or meetup.com for ideas), going out to eat, going to a movie or play, bowling, visiting companies or factories that have tours (or call and ask for one even if they don't publicize them), going to visit local colleges, visiting a pet store (reptiles often are interesting to teen boys), volunteering together, or taking a class.

Classes can be through your parks and recreation department, a community college, or an adult learning center. They don't have to be a big commitment—some last just a few hours. They cover all sorts of topics. Some examples are cooking, computer coding, painting, music, graphic design, all the trades (welding, auto repair, electronic repair, computer repair, etc.), and photography or video editing. The great thing about these activities is that they replace gaming time, and they also expose your child to things that may spark an interest that could turn into a career.

One activity that might surprise you is ballroom dancing. Debra found it appealed to several teen and young adult males on the spectrum. It is highly structured, it has rules, and beginner lessons tend to be very basic, with instructors who go very slowly. The others in the class tend to be welcoming and nonjudgmental. Some communities have regular nights for beginners to drop in early in the evening before more advanced dancers get there.

Duane, a member of AspiesCentral.com, has an interest in amateur radio, and proposed another activity. He pointed out that there are many local amateur radio clubs that enjoy mentoring new members. He finds amateur radio is "stress diverting, self-esteem elevating, safe, wholesome, nonviolent, and loads of fun." There are annual conventions to personally meet on-air friends. He's available to provide help to anyone interested in learning more (you can go to the website and put "amateur radio" in the search box and his posts and responses to it come up). One responder to his post noted that there's much more to the hobby than people realize. She explained that users learn about Morse code, data transmission, satellites, antenna building, and electronics construction, and can collect cards from radio amateurs in other countries. She termed it a "wonderland of exploration."

Relationships with real people in real time can be the best replacement for compulsive gaming. For the people profiled in this book who were headed down the path to obsessive gaming, that was often the key. Jaime said he really curtailed how much he gamed when he moved in with his partner. He said he used to routinely and rather rigidly devote a certain amount of time to gaming, but that once in a relationship this changed and became more fluid. He still spends some time gaming, but says his partner understands and it does not create problems *"as long as I'm aware of my surroundings and how much time I've been playing."*

Get Your Family Interacting

Set aside at least one weeknight and one weekend period for family interaction time. Your child may protest at first, but make it non-negotiable. Chances are they'll come to enjoy the time together. Teens have pride and need to say no to their parents almost automatically. Don't debate with them, or they'll be forced to try to "win" this debate. Speak in a matter-of-fact, calm voice that doesn't put them on the defensive.

Scott and his siblings playing Twister: exercise, skill building, and family fun.

Examples of family activities include playing board games, cooking together, making dessert together, reading together or to each other, playing or making music, drawing together, doing Wii Fit together, working out to a yoga or exercise video together, doing a meditation exercise from a video or online, making slideshows, looking at and talking about old photographs, gardening, learning origami together, finding science experiments online to try, doing puzzles, making stained glass or other crafts, playing cards, having "debates" about current events, reading the newspaper together, playing hide and seek with objects, watching a movie, rearranging furniture, or playing with family pets.

Support Groups

There's not much out there for gaming addiction, and we couldn't find anything specifically for kids on the spectrum. That's going to change as more and more ASD kids who grew up with technology are getting mired in it. We are on the brink of much greater awareness of this problem.

Liz Woolley founded On-Line Gamers Anonymous after the death of her son Shawn in 2002. This group has a website that lists two online chat meetings daily. Some of the meetings are held in voice chat rooms, where participants can actually talk with each other. They also have a site for family and others who want support (much like AA has Alanon). The website is www.olganon.org. Another online recovery group is www.cgaa.info (Computer Gaming Addicts Anonymous).

It's difficult to get addicts off their games and out to a meeting, so most of these groups have struggled to get live groups going. A disadvantage of online meetings is that comments can be inappropriate or cruel at times. An alternative is Narcotics Anonymous. This group has always welcomed addicts of any substance or behavior, and they welcome gamers as well. They have been around long enough to have meetings in most cities, even smaller ones. Their website is www.na.org, and they list meetings on it.

Residential Programs

We could only find one residential program in the United States that works with gaming addicts on the spectrum. It's called ReStart, and it's located in the state of Washington. They treat youth 18 to 28, almost entirely male. We spoke with Dr. Hilarie Cash, one of the founders and Chief Clinical Officer, as well as coauthor of "Video Games and Your Kids." You're probably not going to send your teen off to this program—it's very expensive, not covered by insurance (because internet addiction has not yet been accepted as a medical diagnosis, but that is likely to change), and it only treats five youth at a time. Information about their program, though, may give you some ideas you can use.

Dr. Cash used to recommend that children not play video games until they were 7 years old, but now she says wait until they're 13. "There are many complex things, physically and socially, that children need to learn how to do, and they only learn how to do them by doing them. Video games, which are so mesmerizing, will keep kids locked on a screen rather than doing all these things," she said.

Most of the kids at ReStart come in with diagnoses of ADD, OCD, anxiety, depression, or oppositional defiant disorder. Dr. Cash thinks these are often the *result* of gaming, not the cause, and that ⅓ of the kids actually turn out to be on the autism spectrum. She thinks they were missed because they are high functioning and bright. She finds that depression and anxiety start to dissipate after about 45 to 90 days as "their addicted brains complete withdrawal and return to more normal functioning."

There are two phases to ReStart's program. The first is detox, which takes 45 days minimum with an average length of 55 days. It's not a locked facility, but so far no one has run away. Dr. Cash explains, "These kids don't have much confidence and they are not resourceful. They are not going to initiate and plan leaving. They'd have to catch a bus, or hitchhike, and they have become too dependent to do that."

During the detox phase there are 12-step meetings and individual sessions. Each client has to develop and write out a good plan for a future life where they balance their use of technology. They then present the plan to their peers as well as staff, and keep revising it until it's approved as realistic. It has to include how they're going to deal with triggers, and how they are going to use technology and computers in the future. They also have to identify people who will help keep them accountable. During this period there is a strong emphasis on health, including sleep, diet, and exercise, plus learning basic life skills, like how to cook and clean.

During the second phase of treatment, Cash says, "they're living on their own with someone else in recovery, going back to work and school, and slowly reintroducing computers into their lives. They meet with a private therapist familiar with the program."

The Perspective of One Therapist

We spoke with one of those therapists, Paul Johnson, who estimated about half of the program's clients are on the spectrum. "They naturally perseverate and get really immersed in whatever they do. When you add the socialization problems, it's so much easier for them to let gaming be their social vehicle. The games have so much sensory input, which they love. The sounds, the graphic visuals—some joysticks even vibrate. They feel like they accomplished something. It sucks them in on so many different levels."

Paul acknowledged that treatment is tricky. He said lots of the kids also have ADD or ADHD, and it's really hard for them to self regulate, say "no," and walk away from the game. He thinks visual cues are helpful, as well as exercise and learning to be mindful of triggers and emotions. When they get an impulse to game, he has them sit for 10 minutes first to see if the urge passes.

Even with these techniques, Paul thinks the best way to be successful is to have monitoring software and oversight. He defines success as finding healthy alternatives to gaming and believes the way to that is through forced exposure. He prefers activities that also involve others so that socialization is also learned. He finds activities with lots of sensory input are good, like riding horses, rock climbing, or exercising.

He advises offering as much motivation and reinforcement as possible for your child to engage in other activities: "If you do X, you get Y." (And neither can have anything to do with a computer.)

He also cautions about the dangers of living in college dorms, where gaming is rampant. He suggests looking into colleges that recognize and have support programs for those on the spectrum. They sometimes assign a buddy, who can help with monitoring, and they can assign a private room without computer access.

He acknowledges that relapse is a big problem and says rates are similar to other addictions. He adds, "You can't keep them away from computers. When they get out of the program they have to wean back to healthy levels. They have to use technology even to get a job these days. But again, their software has to be monitored."

He believes three-year-old kids are getting addicted to iPads because parents view them as harmless play. He believes prevention is the key. "If your kid is already addicted, pull the plug and fill their day with other experiences. Just be aware that these kids have become very desperate and will do all sorts of things to get back to their games. You have to be more resourceful than they are. I've had kids go through ceiling crawl spaces to get to their parents' room where the computer is locked up. They'll go use the public library to game. They'll hack through monitoring software."

Summary & Important Points to Remember

✔ Your child isn't motivated to quit gaming. They need a loving push from you because they won't quit on their own.

✔ Their self-concept is by now tied up in gaming, and this is likely the main place they feel mastery and pride.

✔ They may be more emotionally attached to (and attracted to) the online community, virtual friends, and avatars than real people they have to interact with face to face.

✔ Their brain has changed as a result of gaming. They are driven by the powerful intermittent reinforcement of the games, the dopamine rushes, and the intense motivation to achieve higher and higher levels of play.

✔ They have probably neglected basic good habits of diet, exercise, and sleep, and these will need fixing as well.

✔ It's likely they are depressed, stressed, and insecure. They may also feel shame about how much time they have wasted. Their depression may need treatment.

✔ As you intervene, things may get worse before they get better. Some battles you can ignore. It is our opinion that this is not one of them. You need to stick to your guns or their life will stay frozen.

✔ If you've tried to get them to cut back previously but backed off when they gave you flack, they aren't going to believe you're serious this time. Any hint of backing off will make your job much harder.

✔ You may well need professional help with this. If you can't find or afford it, enlist everyone (other relatives, minister, teacher, neighbors) you can think of.

✔ Skill building and exposure to healthy, alternative activities and interests must accompany restrictions.

PART III

Preparing Your Child for Adulthood

CHAPTER 7

Teaching Vital Life Skills
Needed for Success

Tell me and I forget, teach me and I may remember, involve me and I learn.

—*Benjamin Franklin*

We may not be able to prepare the future for our children,

but we can at least prepare our children for the future.

—*Franklin D. Roosevelt*

Children and teens with autism often reach the brink of adulthood grossly unprepared for its demands. For some, this reflects their true limitations. These teens will need significantly modified environments that recognize these limitations while also maximizing abilities. With these in place, they can then lead satisfying, successful lives with continued support from others. They may remain living at home or reside in supervised residential apartments or communities.

Other teens on the spectrum are capable of mastering enough life skills to live independently and find meaningful, financially self-supporting employment. They too may benefit from some modifications, but they're able to handle most skills needed to independently navigate daily life. They're able to complete education that matches their intelligence, secure and maintain meaningful employment, and responsibly manage their finances. They may or may not enter intimate relationships, but they create at least a small cadre of supportive, like-minded work colleagues or friends.

The ultimate achievement of these individuals is that they are not solely consumers of our world's bounty, but in their own unique way they contribute back. This may be as a supportive friend, a valued employee, a member of a community organization, or a loyal volunteer. They may add their creativity to community or family projects, and they view themselves as connected to the world outside themselves.

When teens that are indeed capable of this level of functioning leave adolescence unprepared to step into these roles, they are vulnerable to a crisis. Frustration, anxiety, depression, and regression become significant risks. Too many of our children are reaching adulthood, hitting a wall, and coming to a full stop.

We've introduced you to many teens and adults, and they've shared their stories of navigating these rough seas. You hopefully noticed they have features in common. They continue to overcome learned helplessness, work to develop optimism, find hope through struggle, and use mentors to guide them. In addition, they have been exposed to skill- and character-building in critical areas.

The Four Sets of Skills Each Teenager Must Learn Before Adulthood

Each individual profiled confronted and worked on challenges in four areas: domestic and household skills, driving or using public transit, educational and vocational preparation, and social and community connection. The more guidance, practice, and mastery they acquired in these domains, the easier their movement into adulthood has been.

Parents must lovingly push children in all of these areas. Dr. Mark Klinger, Associate Professor at the University of North Carolina, has studied what helps autistic kids and teens, and advises that parents must ask themselves, "Is this something I need to do for them or is it better for me to just support them?" He advises giving children the opportunity to do absolutely everything that they can independently. "Get them doing the activities now, at home, while you can watch and see what they need help with. Once they move out, it's too late."

Domestic Life and Household Chores

Even if your child shares living space, they will have to handle household chores. The younger your child is when introduced to doing their fair share around the house, the more they'll cooperatively do their part. If a child was never expected to contribute to family chores, they are ill prepared psychologically or practically to suddenly take on this role. In fact, they are likely to resent and avoid it.

Many of the individuals profiled in this book described how important and gratifying early exposure to domestic routines was.

Laura, mother of a creative and employed daughter in her early thirties (who chose to remain anonymous), says she expected a lot from both of her children.

> She was expected to contribute the same as the rest of the family. I always made sure that she had chores that were for the benefit of the whole house, and that she could accomplish them with a reasonable degree of success. We have a quote in our house: "I cannot do everything, but I can do something." We have always lived by that.

Marina's mother, Loretta, recalls having to teach her daughter basics via instruction, repetition, and observation. She also made sure each of her children had chores and that Marina's sisters, two of them older, didn't rescue their younger sibling from her responsibilities.

> I worked night shift. The kids knew what chores they had each day and I could only help so much. They had to make their own beds. One time Marina didn't want to, so she took a needle and took all the threading on her mattress apart. She ended up with basically no mattress! I told her she had to fix it and then make it. Oh boy, the patience that took for each of us. It took her hours to re-stitch what she'd undone but she did it.
>
> Her manners used to be horrible. She held her utensils with her fist. So I had her hold chopsticks, and once she mastered that she went back to using a spoon. I took her fingers and placed them on the spoon and went through the motions. Then I modeled it myself and had her watch. Then I finally had her try it. I would constantly point out others

who were using their utensils correctly and those who were using them incorrectly and point out the difference. I told her she needed to do it properly, not in a barbaric way. I told her it was expected, she could do it, and nobody really cared about how she wanted to do it. There were rules and that was that.

Children Appreciate Parents Who Provide Guidance

You might think that Marina would have rebelled and been angry with her mother, but she makes it clear that she is grateful for her mom's approach.

This has helped me throughout life. It has taught me to have a degree of self-control. I also learned skills.

Marina's hobby of breeding rats is enjoyable and also a way of contributing to her family while she is in college.

Seventeen-year-old Cosette was similarly appreciative of the responsibilities her parents gave her.

My mother and father were probably the largest influences on my life. They encouraged me to embrace my individuality and uniqueness. They taught me what I need to know to be independent. One of the earlier chores I remember was unloading and loading the dishwasher. In the early days, my brother and I switched loading and unloading duties. Although I was never happy about it, it taught me how to use the dishwasher. Later, I learned how to sweep the house on a weekly basis, take out the wastebaskets in all the bathrooms, and clean up after the dogs. In my teen years, I was taught how to run the washing and drying machines, fold and put away my own laundry, and use soap and cleaning fluids on kitchen counters and bathrooms.

Her mom Stephanie had this perspective:

We started her on age-appropriate chores as she grew. Toys put in bins, quilt pulled up on her bed, dishes put in the sink (now in the dishwasher), on to sweeping, dog feeding, and dog poop duty. Yes, she argued, and yes, we quarreled. But the chores got done, and now are habits. When she was small, we tried all the ploys: charts, stickers, rewards, you name it. But she is so smart, she gamed the system every time: "Okay, honey, look, you have 30 tokens to go to Chuck E. Cheese's." "Yay." Tomorrow: "Okay, let's start a new chart." "No, Mommy, I already went to Chuck E. Cheese's." We figured out that more than rewards, it came down to expectations. We had them and they were not negotiable. We knew the fights were worth it.

Cosette now feels she has sufficient skills to maintain her own place with a bit of support. She and her mother have come up with a creative transition plan as Cosette is drawing close to her 18th birthday:

"I do plan to live on my own. I'm moving into a duplex in a few months. My Mom will live on one side and I will live on the other with a roommate. She's a friend from church I've known for several years."

The Value of Family Rituals

Scott's mother devised a family ritual every Saturday evening that taught her son specific skills and incorporated performance standards for each skill.

> Saturday night was "no screen night." Nothing that had a screen could be used. No TV, no movies, no computer, no video games. While weeknights could get hectic, on Saturdays we always ate dinner together as a family and everyone was expected to be there. It was also the one night I always made a dessert. After we finished, each of the three kids, Scott included, had a chore to do related to cleaning up after dinner. The chores rotated each week and they did not get to choose which one they had. They did their assigned task for that week and the other two kids watched to be sure it was done correctly. After all chores were successfully done, we had tea as a family and then we played a board game.

Make Your Approach Fit What Kids on the Spectrum Need

Children on the spectrum learn best by specific, detailed instruction followed by repeated practice. They're not likely to automatically learn the mundane but necessary tasks of daily life without our intentionally providing meticulous information and training. Also, since they often have little curiosity about the world outside their special interests, they seldom come to us and ask us to teach them a skill.

One of the goals of Patrick's counseling was to get him up to speed on age-appropriate life skills. He was usually sent home with a list of tasks that he agreed to try before his next appointment. His parents were on board and periodically joined sessions to evaluate progress and stay on task. His father taught him how to take care of the yard, both parents helped with driving and cooking skills, and his mom taught him to do his own laundry.

> We took it step by step. When he first starting mowing, there'd be missed grass between each row. I told him not to worry about it—just

go back and fix it. Now he does it very well. When he started to cook, we did simple things like hotdogs, burritos, and steak on the barbeque. When he gets used to what he's done, we introduce something new and we help him.

He was sure driving was impossible at first. (Everything is impossible at first.) Now he drives on the freeway over to another town! He stops at each stop sign and counts to three before proceeding. And he yells at me if I unbuckle the seat belt before we come to a complete stop: "Dad!"

Nancy, Daniel's mom, realizes that her son needs extra help with household skills.

Daniel is very compliant but he needs specific instructions. If he doesn't feel like he knows what to do, he won't do anything. In college he tried to be a good roommate by taking out the trash. He knows that's not a chore other people like to do, but he doesn't have a sense of smell so it doesn't bother him. Other than that, he needs to be told what to do. He likes people to communicate very clearly with him.

Don't Take Anything for Granted—Break Tasks Down and Tell Them the Rules

An approach that works well is to first make a list of all the tiny components of the task before attempting to teach it. The large number of steps involved will probably surprise you because you take them for granted. Assume that your teen takes nothing for granted. Once you have the steps clearly defined, put them into groups; otherwise, too many items on a list are overwhelming. As an extra organizational aid, use colored markers to designate first steps in each sequence.

First, they need to watch you do each step. Explain every action. In addition to verbal instruction, put it in writing for future reference. It is a good idea to put them on laminated index cards, and post them where the task occurs. If you have the habit of repeatedly verbally reminding your child of things, they probably just regard it as nagging. Visual prompts help break this pattern. Your child will still come to you instead of reading the prompt. Don't give in and reinforce helplessness. Simply direct them back to the visual instructions. If they really need help, make them tell you what specific question they have that is not answered on the index card.

If you don't teach your child these skills methodically and early, kids with autism are unlikely to figure them out on their own. For example, whereas a NT college freshman who never had to do laundry at home will probably ask another student for help; this may not even occur to a young adult with autism. They may simply wear the same soiled clothes day after day instead of soliciting assistance.

Kids with autism don't automatically generalize. You might assume that if they learned, for instance, that the pizza delivery guy expects a tip, they'd realize that the barber does too, since they are both service providers. You'd likely be wrong unless you clearly state and explain "the rule." Have them join you in coming up with the rules—if they are able to figure out some of them themselves, they are more likely to remember and internalize those. Write down the rules for visual thinkers.

An Example from Temple

When we were talking about how important it is to break down tasks into steps and that ASD kids can't make use of a long string of verbal instructions, Temple recalled a specific time this was absolutely necessary for her.

> When I was in graduate school I worked at a dairy. It was my job to set up the milking equipment, milk the cows, and then clean up. There are a lot of steps involved in those tasks. The dairy had a checklist on the wall with all the steps spelled out. That saved me. I would have been in big trouble without it.
>
> Milking cows wasn't the problem. But there were so many other steps: I had to turn on the refrigeration. I had to put the filter in and set up the pipes. There were four or five things to clean. I had to remember to take the hose out of the milk tank. And if I did one thing wrong, I could wreck a whole tank of milk because soapy water could get into that tank.
>
> I'm not unique. You absolutely cannot give an ASD kid a long string of verbal instructions and expect them to succeed. You have to

pretend they are an airline pilot and you have to provide them the sort of checklist all pilots have to go through before each flight. Make it in the form of bullet points. Put them in the exact sequence you want them done. Then your child can be successful.

Regular Chores Help Your Child

Martha, who has found a job she enjoys and is respected for, still struggles in the domestic realm. When asked what childhood tasks or chores helped her prepare for adulthood, she couldn't think of anything specific other than being expected to keep her room clean. Yet she says she seldom did. When asked how she's doing now with household maintenance, she described it as a significant challenge. It hasn't become a routine habit for her. It's reasonable to wonder, if she had received more consistent loving pushes as a child, if this area would be easier now.

Keeping a clean house has been a huge struggle all my life. I have not gotten to the point of classic hoarding, but I always have more stuff than I have places to put it away. It seems like my apartment gets dirty overnight and I put off cleaning until I am about to have company. I really hate housework and cleaning up dirty dishes. So I eat a lot of frozen meals and treat myself to meals out usually once or twice a week. My brother comes for a visit about every six to eight weeks and this gives me a good incentive to clean up regularly.

Similarly, Jaime, who has obtained a good job and is in a committed relationship, had little to say when asked about childhood household responsibilities. He mentioned that his mother did make him watch his diet and restricted him from sodas. He has clearly incorporated these lessons and they have become routines. He goes to the gym at his work "every single workday" and takes circuit training and "boot camp" classes. Yet he has relied on his girlfriend for many household instructions, including cooking.

I taught myself the basics of cooking for myself—eggs, pasta, that sort of thing. However, my partner taught me how to use a slow cooker, how to use spices and mix flavors and so on. We also started watching cooking competition shows like "Cutthroat Kitchen" and those shows presented cooking in such an entertaining fashion that I absorbed the information willingly.

Sarah, who learned much from her neighbor Armida, nevertheless realizes that the lack of regular chores at home impacted her development. She said she still struggles with cooking and cleaning. She is continually improving her skills with the help of her husband, workshops, and books.

I had a disruptive childhood, which slowed my growth as an early adult. I had very little structure, routine, or predictability at home. There were no consistent chores or tasks in my house throughout my childhood. I learned primarily from my neighbor. Now that I know my diagnosis, it gives me great hope and my life has improved. I appreciate knowing there are resources (people, books, workshops, and groups) out there that offer training, encouragement, and hope for improving my skills.

Getting Around Independently: Driving or Using Public Transportation

Driving is one of the main milestones many NT teens welcome to increase their sense of autonomy and freedom. Most parents of these teens, while initially nervous, are generally excited and relieved when their child can transport themselves (and younger siblings) for a change. Some adolescents on the autism spectrum are also excited to learn to drive, but many are primarily anxious, often to the point of delaying or refusing getting a license. Their parents frequently have concerns about safety, so they're prone to reinforce their teen's hesitation.

Driving requires both cognitive and motor skills. It's not simply a matter of intelligence. Memory, attention, flexibility, and reflexes all play a part in how safely someone drives. Some teens with autism are impaired enough in these areas that they cannot pass the driver's exam, and the decision to forego a license is prudent. Others simply need more time, as they are developmentally a few years behind. These teens may not be ready right at 16. They may not even be ready until they are in their 20s.

You Have to Address Their Fears

Psychological factors are the biggest stumbling block for other teens. They resist novelty, are afraid of making mistakes, and hate the unpredictability that comes with driving (weather, unknown routes, and other, unpredictable drivers). Many prefer dependence over autonomy, which creates their greatest challenge. Parents should not automatically give in to these fears. They are not deal breakers, though they do need to be addressed.

If your teen is resisting getting a license, insist on a frank conversation about their reasons. Unless they have shown substantial cognitive and motor impairment in other areas, be wary of new concerns suddenly being brought up now. They're likely a cover for fear or apathy. In this case, your teen desperately needs a loving push. Without a driver's license, your child is more likely to become a recluse at home and much more likely to become a compulsive computer user or gamer.

Daniel, 25, does not have his driver's license. He actually obtained his permit, but said he didn't spend enough time practicing, so he wasn't ready to take the exam by the time it expired. He acknowledged that he didn't do much practice driving because of both anxiety and lack of motivation. Yet he explained that with more push from others, he might now be licensed, and he said if he had children he would push them to drive.

> I didn't get much push from my parents to practice. You need two people to practice driving. I didn't push them and they didn't push me."

To get places, he mainly relies on others such as his brother, who is also his roommate, or he walks where he needs to go. His mom's hope was that he would learn to use his local public transit system, but when interviewed, Daniel didn't seem interested in learning this on his own.

A Push Plus *LOTS* of Practice = Success

In contrast, when a push is combined with extra practice, support, and customized instruction, many teens that were adamantly against or terrified of driving now do it routinely and successfully. Patrick, who now regularly and casually drives locally and to his out of town voice-over coach, initially hated the idea of driving and wanted nothing to do with it. Months of counseling appointments included discussing his distorted concerns, which on the surface combined disdain for other drivers and a world that relies on automobiles, but covered a genuine fear of the unfamiliar and of making a mistake on the road.

Debra and Patrick could have discussed it forever, though, and Patrick would still not be driving if it weren't for the consistent efforts of his Aunt Mary. She taught him actual driving skills, as well as how to shift his attitude, be more flexible, and cope with unexpected situations.

We'd go driving every Wednesday and every day I had off. We drove for two hours at a time this way for an entire year. He was very anxious, and he also had a typically autistic way of distorting the intentions of other drivers. He would say things like "That driver just wanted to mess up my day," and I would explain that no, that driver did that because he needed to merge.

I tried to constantly put him in situations that would stretch him. One time when I picked him up I parked illegally on purpose and honked the horn—he had to quickly run over and get in the car. He had to respond and not just stand there. Another time I was driving with him in the car and I had to look up directions. I stopped in an alley and he went berserk because that's against the rules and I wasn't following the letter of the law. He yelled "NO, NO, NO, Mary!" and I yelled back "STOP!" but my voice cracked when I did it. We both sat there for a minute kind of stunned (we don't yell at each other)—and then we both cracked up laughing. He is used to me putting him in off-the-cuff situations. I've tried to introduce that into his life.

Teens on the Spectrum Can Be Especially Safe Drivers!

Studies suggest that teens on the spectrum may be among our safer drivers. One study found that only 12% of a group of teen drivers with autism had received citations. This compares to the California DMV statistics that show rates of citations ranging from 31 to almost 40% for 16- to 19-year-old teens in general. Since a characteristic of autism is preference for routine, once our teens learn the rules of the road they follow them carefully and consistently. They tend to find excessive speed and risk-taking offensive, which is unfortunately not typical of NT teens. They are also less likely to drive in groups with other teens, which is a situation that creates dangerous peer pressure for risk-taking in NT adolescents. Finally, with fewer social contacts plus a preferred focus on doing only one thing at a time, they are less likely to call or text while driving.

In fact, most of the risk factors listed by the CDC are unlikely to be present for drivers on the spectrum. For example, only about 50% of teens in general say they wear seat belts when riding with someone else. In male drivers, 37% were speeding at the time of an accident and 25% had been drinking. Alcohol was implicated in 23% of fatalities involving teens of both sexes, and 71% of those drinking teens were not wearing a seat belt. Most (53%) accidents involving teens occur on Friday, Saturday, or Sunday. These risk factors are not going to be high for autistic youth.

You might be surprised which two factors most determine whether teens on the spectrum get their driver's license. They have nothing to do with attributes of the teen: Students more likely to get their driver's license had IEPs that specifically included driving goals, and parents who had already taught one or more teen to drive.

Whether a child is capable of driving or instead needs to learn to use public transit, the approach is the same. Start with the basics, go slowly, and practice over and over (and over!).

Temple's Mantra: Burn Up an Entire Tank of Gas Practicing!

Temple learned to drive one summer at her aunt's ranch. For that entire hot summer she just drove the ranch's temperamental three-on-the-floor stick shift pickup truck back and forth down the dusty lane to the mailbox. That was a six-mile round trip each day!

I had to drive there six days a week. The first couple of times, my aunt drove but I steered from the passenger seat. Then I tried it. And boy, did that truck have a nasty clutch! I'd pop it and it'd lurch forward five or six feet—but there was nothing out there for it to hit so it didn't matter. We didn't have cell phones then, so I had to figure it out myself if I stalled. By the end of the summer, I'd driven 200 miles on that dirt lane! By then I'd acquired confidence and skill.

My career in the livestock industry would not be possible if I was unable to get around independently. Not driving is going to limit lots of kids work wise. Just go slow. Let them use up a tank of gas before they even start driver's education, because in driver's education they take them out too fast.

There are many places you can burn up that tank of gas that are isolated and safe. Deserted country roads, dry open fields, or empty parking lots all work. Colleges or large office complexes are other good choices. You can go to one of the big discount stores before they open or after they close, and set up cones or other homemade obstacles to practice steering around. Practice braking in front of them and backing up to them, also.

Drivers Education Has to Be Different for Spectrum Teens

If your teen has an IEP, insist that driver's training be formally included in it. Then make sure the training is suited to your teen. Most driver education classes move way too fast for the autistic teen, taking them into traffic much too soon. If the instructor is impatient, insist on another, as the teacher has to be calm, reassuring, and not intimidating. Each new driving task must be broken into steps, and each step needs to be addressed one at a time. Your teen won't be able to learn, otherwise. Instructors unfamiliar with autism need to be explicitly told that if a student with autism becomes angry or oppositional they are probably overwhelmed and afraid, and need a quiet break. The instructor needs to stop talking and stop giving them more information at that point. Tasks should also be presented in a logical sequence, with a consistent approach. Lessons should occur frequently and regularly. Instructors should use keywords and direct language.

Your teen may also need explicit instruction in areas that NT teens pick up by observation or intuitiveness. Another child may have watched to see how you pump and pay for gas or clean the windshield, but your spectrum teen may not have noticed. A neurotypical teen may automatically have a hunch why an on-coming driver is flashing their lights. They can come up with possible scenarios such as the other driver is warning them about police radar or an accident ahead, or trying to tell them their high beams are on. An ASD driver, however, may need this explained explicitly.

Some teens on the autism spectrum struggle with spatial awareness, and these teens will find it difficult to accurately judge distances. Instructors can use non-standard approaches with these students. Instead of telling them, for instance, how far to stay back from other cars, or how close to the curb to park by using measurements, they can use visual images.

Private driving instructors are usually well worth the expense if you can afford it. Some kids are fine with learning from their parents. Others really want someone else. In that case, if a paid instructor is out of the question, try to find another relative, neighbor, or community or church member who can be your kid's "driving coach."

In addition to teaching technical skills, driving coaches should repeatedly role-play "what-if" situations that might fluster an autistic teen. Some of these situations involve actual driving, such as what to do when a pedestrian enters the street or when a motorcycle splits lanes near your car. Others involve non-driving scenarios such as being pulled over by a police officer, having a flat tire, or being involved in a fender-bender. While all teens would benefit from role-playing these scenarios, they are more important for teens with autism, whose anxiety and lack of social awareness can complicate an unexpected situation.

All Role-Playing Must Break Down Each Step

Get really super-specific in your role-playing. For example, if you're acting out what to do if the police pull your car over, there are many, many steps you have to break down and give detailed instructions for. First, explain to them why the officer might stop them. They need to know it doesn't always mean they've done anything wrong or are in trouble. Tell them never to run from the officer or to touch the officer. Don't simply tell them to "be polite"—instead, spell out exactly what you mean. Tell them to roll down the window when the officer approaches. Tell them to use the term "Officer" when speaking. Practice it with them. Tell them to do exactly what the officer asks, and to keep their hands on the wheel at the 10 and 2 o'clock positions. Explain that they are doing this so the officer can see their hands. Tell them to tell the officer everything they are doing to do before they do it. For example, if the officer asks for their registration and it is in the glove compartment, have them practice saying, "My registration is in the glove compartment. May I get reach over and get it out for you, Officer?" If their license happens to be in their backpack in the trunk, they need to know to tell the officer that, not just get out of the car.

These instructions may seem like overkill, but for a youth on the spectrum they're not. Most police officers are unfamiliar with autism and they won't know how to interpret any unexpected behavior. Situations can escalate if each party is confused by the other or nervous. Take your time with your teen and prepare them fully. You might want to print up and laminate a small card explaining that your teen is autistic and have them hand it to the officer. Just remember they have to keep the card close by and tell the officer they are reaching for it before making sudden moves. Again, this needs to be role-played until done automatically.

Finally, explain to your child that if they are stopped at night, the officer will probably shine a flashlight into their car. Let them know this is routine. Also let them know that it is possible that the officer will have a siren or their flashing lights on. They may even have a police dog with them.

One Canadian police department has a page on their website www.brockville-police.com called "What to Expect When Stopped by Police." You may want to review it with your teen. It is always a good idea to present information to ASD kids in writing as well as verbally. Especially when there are multiple steps or things to remember, regard this as a necessity.

Rules are Good—Spell Them Out!

Once you've burned up that first tank of gas off road, and your teen is ready to drive on a real road, first sit down and go over "driving rules." Write them down and make sure your teen can repeat them back to you. General good rules for beginner drivers on the spectrum will include: People will not talk to me while I am driving unless it is related to my driving or a matter of safety, neither driver nor passengers will talk on the phone, the radio will not be on, and I will do a practice run whenever possible before driving to a new place if I have an appointment at a specific time. This helps tremendously as the anxiety of having to be somewhere new at a certain time can cause your teen to be flustered.

If your teen is in counseling, a CBT approach lends itself well to preparation for driving. In addition to shifting distorted fears to more realistic perspectives, a therapist can teach your teen specific calming techniques to use while learning, as well as later during the examination. They can also remind the teen of how much progress they are making, which often has to come from an outsider, as those with autism may lack this perspective, plus they tend to over-focus on what they have not achieved.

Scott is a good example of an approach that worked well.

I had mandatory driver's ed at school, plus my mom took me to a local community college when no one was around and the parking lot was empty. We took the family minivan and she showed me the parts of it and really broke it down: "Here is the brake pedal, here is the gas pedal." She'd have me try things and explain exactly what was happening. I remember she had me try to go forward with the parking brake on and then said, "Hear that noise? That is a bad thing," and explained it. She told me to turn left and told me to notice exactly how sharply the car turned. She explained that was the turning radius and why it was important to know. She walked me through all of the basic mechanical processes of the car. It was Mom's patient tutorial that really helped.

Scott and his mom

How to Learn Public Transit if Your Child Is Not Ready or Able to Drive

Even if your teen is not yet ready for driving, these same principles apply to learning to navigate public transit. Cosette, who is approaching her 18th birthday, doesn't feel ready to drive yet, and her mother accepts that. She has not practiced at all, and she seems to realize that fear may be her biggest hurdle:

> I have these ridiculous scenarios in my head. But the 'mights' are probably more powerful than they should be, and I know the anticipation is the worst. The 'what ifs' are the worst.

Cosette's mother has consequently made sure her daughter is able to use local buses to get herself to school and other places.

> The week before I started going to community college my mom took me on the bus every day. We would ride from home to school and then back home. I needed to learn how to signal the driver that I wanted to get off, and I had to learn which stop was mine. The first couple of days my mom would tell me when to pull the 'stop' strap but then she made me do it myself. Once I learned how to get to school, she helped me learn to take the bus to other places. We practiced, plus she showed me how the routes are on the bus website and I learned to read them. Now I go alone to school, the library, my friend's house, and the mall.

Educational and Vocational Preparation

There is a wide range of intellectual and vocational capability represented on the autism spectrum, but there are common pathways that help all spectrum youth reach their fullest capacity. Remembering how overwhelming a typical classroom environment can be for those with autism serves as a foundation for good, realistic planning. Sensory overload is common, and can cause great anxiety, problems focusing, and what may mistakenly appear to be oppositional behavior. Teachers in mainstream classes, who are still usually unfamiliar with autism, can compound the child's struggle by using approaches that actually make their distress worse.

Gifted children are often bored in class, while others with uneven abilities confuse instructors, who don't understand how a child can do so well in one class, yet so poorly in another. They may attribute the uneven performance to personality or behavioral problems instead of knowing that this is typical in autism. They're also commonly perplexed and frustrated by children who seem to know material, yet can't respond in the classroom or on assignments in the same way neurotypical children. Slower processing time, having difficulty putting thoughts into words, and struggles with open-ended writing assignments are common areas of misunderstanding.

Many students in the higher functioning range of the autism spectrum still need intensive educational assistance. Yet because testing may show average intellect, some schools refuse to provide IEPs, special education classes as needed, or accommodations. As we said in chapter two, going above the child's specific school to local school district personnel is sometimes necessary, and awareness of the classification of "Other Health Impaired" has helped many parents get their child the help they needed and deserved. Other parents decided their child would be best served by changing schools, or by being home schooled. Many students profiled in chapter one benefited greatly from either accommodations or alternate educational settings.

If your school didn't have any ideas or experience with providing transition services, you can give them information about Project SEARCH, a model transition program that has been used to help youth with ASD gain competitive employment. Their website address is projectsearch.us. The program contains the following components:

- Identifying job skill strengths, preferences, and interests
- Communicating with supervisors and coworkers
- Dressing and behaving professionally
- Communicating with customers
- Practicing specific work skills
- Accepting correction
- Asking for and taking a break
- Calling in sick or late, or requesting time off
- Preparing a résumé
- Attending a job interview

You May Have to Educate the Teachers

Patrick's father, Ray, said they decided to switch their son to a private junior and senior high school. Even then they learned they had to take the initiative to make sure his teachers were aware of his son's unique needs.

> I'm a working-class guy and Patrick's mom, who is also on the spectrum, is a homemaker and wasn't capable of home schooling. So even though it stretched us, we had to make it happen. We thought having smaller classes and being able to stay with the same kids in each class might be a good idea. The school tried to do their best for us, but we still had to educate them. I remember we gave them reading materials. That helped.

The parental advocacy required to secure resources took a great deal of time and effort for the parents of these students. Watching their child suffer and doubting their efforts when they were repeatedly met with resistance often marked their journey. Michelle's daughter "Suzanne," now in her early 30s, got her high school diploma after being home schooled and has gone on to hold satisfying long-term jobs. Her mom recalls two incidents that each left a lasting impact.

> We had the biggest problems with her IEPs. The goals they set were ridiculously low. This is why I home schooled her for high school. The worst thing a professional ever said to me was during an IEP in about fifth grade. I was concerned that the plan didn't include working on her reading. I was told, "We would all like our children to be white collar workers; however, some of them are just meant to be blue collar workers."
>
> But we have also been fortunate to have some amazing teachers come into our lives. Trying to figure out how to reach her and help her was so overwhelming for all concerned. I had four specific people who encouraged me to follow my heart and my gut, and not to worry about what might be conventional. I knew this is what I wanted to do, but their encouragement gave me the confidence to do it. I once was having a bit of a meltdown myself in a school supervisor's office, and when I was finished I was embarrassed and sad that I had acted that

way I had. I will never forget her response: "Don't ever apologize for being your child's advocate. I wish there were more parents like you." It gave me the strength to keep going.

Don't Be Afraid to Request a Change of Teachers or Classes

If your child is bored in a class because it's too easy, request a meeting with the teacher and ask for more stimulating material. Find out if there is an option for advanced placement or a different teacher. Some teachers are burned out or just not good. Do your best to get your child out of their classroom. Go up the ladder to the principal or school district if possible.

On the other hand, don't coddle your child just because they're complaining. Make sure they have a legitimate grievance and aren't just running away from a strict teacher or someone they don't click with.

We encourage you to do whatever you can to get your child in classes with teachers who really care, are creative, and inspire your child. You've already read about how very important teachers were to many of the people profiled in this book. Some of our brightest and most successful adults owe their achievements in part to high school teachers. When Temple visited Fermi Lab, a United States Department of Energy national laboratory specializing in high-energy particle physics, half of the scientists told her they became interested in physics because they were exposed to a great teacher in high school.

In Some Ways, College May Be Easier Than High School— Some Examples

It is not uncommon for students who eventually attend college to struggle mightily earlier in their education. Several of the students profiled here, including Sarah, were good examples.

I struggled with not knowing why I was different in school cognitively. I had major struggles with reading comprehension. I also had very difficult struggles with writing essays. I had difficulty following complex, multi-tasked instructions, understanding concept-level topics, and thinking in analogies, similes, and metaphors. I'd read something and come up with some weird, different, and odd conclusion about the story I read. I remember in an English class summarizing a part of a Shakespeare play enthusiastically, hastily, and differently than the teacher and other students, and I was laughed at. I was teased for being weird.

I was not diagnosed yet but my mom and I suspected something was different in my brain. This suspicion led me in junior college to get tested for a learning disability. But this only yielded poor reading comprehension and nothing else.

Note that Sarah is 36, and screening for autism spectrum was not routinely done back when she was a college student. There are patterns on IQ or learning disability testing that are common for those on the spectrum, but they probably wouldn't have been looked for nor recognized at that time. Sarah was not diagnosed until she was 32.

Fortunately, though, Sarah had several inspiring, gifted teachers who helped keep her enthusiasm for learning strong, and her interest focused on the subjects she later turned into a vocation. She says she focused on staying positive and persistent. In spite of her many struggles, she completed high school, attended junior college, and then completed her B.A. in Environmental Science.

Sarah works as a wildlife biologist, a career that evolved from an early interest in nature and was influenced by several mentors.

Scott, who is in his late 20s, also struggled in the classroom. His mom Katie described how his problems showed up by preschool, continued off and on, and were the worst in high school. Even though he had made two friends in earlier school years, he said high school was "hell." His best friend rejected him because Scott wasn't interested in experimenting with drugs. He started spending lunch period in the library. It was his worst social stage.

College, though, was a different and better experience altogether. Part of the reason was likely due to the particular college Scott attended. It was small, religiously affiliated, and had a terrible sports program, so there were few jocks there. Scott's mom noted, "Jocks find AS kids the most irritating."

The professors there were more into teaching than research. They were readily available to help students. They also routinely worked with the disability office and took into consideration the unique challenges of each student.

Cosette too found college much better than high school:

> College is pretty good. The people actually care. High school people don't care—they're always talking and disruptive, and I couldn't focus. They're always talking about 'dude … !' In college, though, they want to engage and have a real discussion. They pay attention. They don't talk as loud or as much; I guess because it costs. It's just a better environment. Plus I don't have to get up so early!"

While college or trade school is much smoother than high school for many young adults on the spectrum, unfortunately some who are capable of higher education don't want anything more to do with school. With the trauma of high school still fresh in their mind, some teens are adamantly against additional education. They assume it will be the same grueling, bullying, confidence-eroding experience. Or they try it and bomb out after one semester because no one helped them select appropriate classes or provided guidance. A loving push, combined with starting small and making wise choices about the school and the classes, can make a huge difference.

Parents often wait until after high school or college to start thinking about a job for their child. This is way too late. By early childhood, you can discern the special interests of some kids. By middle school, most children with autism are giving clear indications of their thinking style and what type of work they'll be best suited for. That's the time to encourage children to find activities that match their interests and to let them run with it. It's also the time to expose them to new experiences that may capture their interest.

Great Practical Advice from a College Professor

We asked Dr. Mark Klinger, who was one of the founders of the University of Alabama's College and Transition Support Program, what factors predicted success for ASD students. This program, one of the first in the United States to form a support program specifically for kids on the spectrum, pairs each ASD student with a peer mentor for twice weekly check-in meetings. He found that the more prepared the student was to handle basic, everyday skills, the better they did. He found that the kids who had practiced household chores and self-care while they were in high school made the transition, while others failed: "Therapists and parents have been focusing on social skills and have made efforts to get their kids into groups. That's good, but there are more important interventions. Parents and professionals need to focus on skills related to independence and being able to manage the basics of daily life. The kids who don't already have these skills are going to have a really hard time. Many of them end up in their dorm rooms playing video games 24/7, quit going to classes, and end up failing."

He has four recommendations for parents:

1. **Get your kids doing household and personal care tasks on their own.** For each task, instead of automatically doing it for them, ask yourself if this is really something they can't learn to do themselves. Give them the opportunity to do everything independently that they can. You can be supportive, but doing it for them backfires.

   A specific example he gave was that kids arrive at college never having gotten into the habit of getting themselves up in the morning by using an alarm clock. Instead, mom went into their bedroom, coaxed them out of bed, and told them what to do: go get breakfast, go get dressed, and so on. These kids are totally capable of doing this themselves, but there's not going to be anyone at college to teach them. By then it's usually too late.

   A second example Dr. Klinger gave was that kids come to college and haven't yet developed good hygiene habits. If mom always reminded them to shower, and now she's not there, they're going to run into trouble with others because they're going to alienate and offend them. He said more than one mentor has had to tell their student "You stink." They need rules for how often they should do every personal hygiene task: showering, brushing their teeth, shampooing, and so on.

2. **Get your kid used to having and using an independent organizational aid.** These kids are usually very disorganized and unless remedied, this is a disaster. They need something to prompt them to get stuff done and show up. They can use paper and pencil, a planner, a programmed smart phone, or a computer (Google calendar can be set up to automatically text them the day before a test, or a week before a paper is due, or half an hour before each class). He notes that most ASD students are rule based enough that if they get a text saying they have to be at class in 30 minutes, they will go.

3. **Teach your kid to know how to ask for help.** Have them practice until it's comfortable. Social initiation is really hard for these kids, and they have to have this skill because they're going to have times they need to ask their professor (or employer) for help. The other person isn't going to come to them. They have to be able to self-advocate and they have to know how to go up to their professor after class or how to schedule a meeting for later. It's critical, because when ASD kids get behind in a class, they're embarrassed and they stop going. They have too much anxiety to go back once they've missed a couple of days.

4. **Make sure your child's mood is stable.** It really matters a lot. Untreated depression and anxiety are highly linked to unsuccessful outcome after high school. This should be taken care of before your child leaves home or gets a job. If your child takes medication, they have to already be in the habit of taking it without a reminder. Again, if mom always reminded them, they're going to come to college and soon spiral down emotionally because they're skipping doses or they stop taking it altogether. Plus they need to know what to do when there are only a few pills left in the bottle; most have never refilled their prescriptions themselves. They need to be able to handle this or they simply stop taking their meds once they run out.

Kids Need to Be Exposed to Practical Trades

Most of today's schools have sadly eliminated hands-on classes like shop and home economics, as well as the creative arts. These days kids come out of high school unable to build or fix things, or ever having been exposed to trades. This is an especially great disadvantage to our teens whose brains are wired visually and may want to pursue trade or technical jobs that don't require a four-year degree.

Since the schools aren't doing it, it falls to parents and mentors to provide loving pushes that get kids out and prepare them for the world of work. Help them find part-time jobs in the neighborhood like mowing lawns, or helping to set up for community events. Work alongside them if needed. These kids win the trifecta—they acquire confidence, practical skills, and better social competence.

Temple's Path to Employment

Temple's "job" history is a great example of how a little creativity can go a long way in helping your child. It's not super important *what* your child does. It's just important that they get out of the house and have some responsibility and learn the necessary skills that go with any job. It doesn't matter if the "job" pays or not, but if it does, be sure you take that opportunity to teach your child how to manage money. If it's a volunteer position, it still prepares them to handle the most important things: showing up on time, following instructions, and having enough confidence to do the job.

Temple wrote earlier about how her mother expected all her children to learn appropriate social skills by being "party hosts" starting at around age seven. That counted as a "job" because it taught her the fundamental lessons of doing your best and making a contribution.

Temple also helped a neighbor, who was a seamstress. She'd go over to her house and help by tearing out the old hems in garments the woman was mending. It didn't matter that she had no intention of becoming a seamstress herself—that's not the point of early experiences. She learned valuable basics like being there when she said she would, paying attention, and listening to instructions. She also learned an important lesson about making mistakes. One day, while using a seam ripper, she tore the fabric of the garment she was working on. She was mortified and afraid to admit what happened. When she did, she learned a valuable attitude and approach to mistakes. First, we all make them. Second, it's our job to try to fix them. Her neighbor showed her how to correct the mistake, and she continued on.

By her teen years, Temple got a whopping $10 for painting a sign for a lady who owned a beauty shop. Temple knew the woman's husband, because he did construction nearby and she enjoyed talking to him and watching him work. It's these simple connections that can lead to opportunities to stretch your child. The more people you and your child interact with, the more opportunities.

Temple and one of the signs she painted.

At her aunt's ranch, where she spent summers during high school and college, Temple waited tables, cleaned horse stalls, and took guests on trail rides. During college, she had an internship where she worked in a lab. She also worked as a helper with autistic kids, playing croquet and flying kites with them, and supervising them in the pool.

While she was getting her master's degree at Arizona State University, she worked as a cattle chute operator. She also built on her earlier sign painting and got a paid gig painting the sign for the "Himalayan Monster" exhibit at the Arizona State Fair. (The "monster" was a wax dummy in a freezer chest full of ice!)

She made up a portfolio of the signs she'd painted and walked up to an old sign painter named Pat, who told her she was using the wrong kind of brush. He showed her the correct kind, and gave her more paid work. She painted the sign for the "Country Western Wax Museum" ticket booth at the fair, and also the booth sign for the fair's "it slices, it dices!" knife hawker.

She later started writing for the *Arizona Farmer-Rancher* after she nervously approached the editor at a cattle auction. That first anxious encounter resulted in her inaugural article, then regular columns, and finally her becoming the livestock editor.

Give Your Child Similar Experiences: Two Real Examples

Story #1: Dog Walking and Flower Designing

Many of the kids profiled here benefited from these sorts of experiences. Michelle's daughter "Suzanne" is a good example. Her mom tells how she exposed her to the world of work:

> I home schooled her for high school and worked with her on practical skills throughout the day. I was self-employed, so she would sit across the desk from me and work on her schoolwork and ask me questions. As I photocopied or filed, she would do the same with her work. She often listened to work phone conversations I had. After I hung up, I'd explain what had just been discussed and why. I took her everywhere with me, including clients' offices, and she had to interact with everyone I did every day. It worked well because instead of feeling like a child being forced to interact with people, she felt like she was my assistant, learning how to represent ourselves to clients and vendors.

Suzanne started a dog-walking service as a teenager. She said that helped her get used to the idea of being self-employed and taught her to count money. It also helped her socially because while it was hard for her to talk to people, it was easier when they had dogs to talk about.

After high school, Suzanne's mother worked very hard to find an apprenticeship opportunity for her daughter. She felt Suzanne was naturally talented working with and arranging flowers. She finally found a flower designer willing to take her daughter on a training basis. This turned out to be very successful and evolved into a job that lasted 10 years, until the business was sold.

Finding her daughter unemployed, her mom got creative once again. Recalling her self-employment as a dog walker and the fact that she'd done some flower arranging on her own, she had business cards printed up saying Suzanne was self-employed.

> That way she wasn't presenting herself as an unemployed person looking for a job. This gave her the self-confidence to get herself out there. The result was that she was offered a job with a large chain, and now she is working ¾ time and supplementing her income with her self-employed activities.

This is a great example of a loving push. Her daughter still had to get out there and interview, and she's the one who needs to get up and get to work now, but a creative, proactive push on her mom's part helped her get there.

Story #2: From a Corn Festival to 20,000 Potential Customers

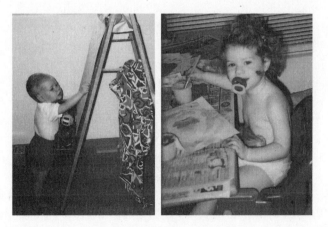

Special interests can appear very early and be nurtured into a career.

Cosette just turned 18 but has been drawing since she was a toddler. In elementary school friends were hard to come by, and her art skills helped. Her peers loved it when she would draw pictures at their request. Since then, she moved on to selling simple $1.00 drawings to children at the Davis Ranch Corn Festival, then to being a vendor at the Sacramento Convention Center, where 20,000 attendees are expected at this year's Anime Convention.

She got there with lots of guidance from her mom, an idea from her brother, encouragement from other vendors she talked to, and plenty of practice and experimentation on her part. Her mom outlined some of the steps Cosette took.

I make crafts myself and I was going to sell jewelry at a small local festival last summer (the Corn Festival). I told Cosette she could put her drawings there too. My idea was just for her to give them away—they were very simple index cards with pictures of baby dragons, winged horses, and unicorns—that sort of thing. I figured it would be good socialization practice. Well, she came back with a better idea. She said "Okay, let's give them away, but if they want them colored in, it will cost them $1.00!" She also came up with the idea that the kids could ask her to draw their favorite character or animal and she'd do a quick 30" sketch for $1.00.

Well, the kids LOVED the idea and were running back to their parents asking for that dollar all day! She made $110.00 that first day, which included some tips, because she had seen another vendor do well with a tip jar, so she put her own out. I, on the other hand, didn't sell a darn thing that day!

Then Cosette researched using social media to post some of her drawings. She found Tumblr, a site where anyone can post any kind of media and have their own mini-blog of sorts. She posted silly pictures of cats or images from Doctor Who. She hasn't done that much lately, though, because she said there were too many trolls on that site (obnoxious people who stir up trouble online).

Her brother had posted some art on DeviantArt, which bills itself as the largest online art gallery and community, and suggested Cosette try that. So she started to use that as her own virtual art gallery. Later she got onto Etsy, the huge online store, through me. Many years ago I had a virtual store on that site, and your account never goes away, so she started using it.

After the Corn Festival, she wanted to sell at other festivals and fairs. Comic-Con was coming to Sacramento, so we rented a booth. She sold $250 worth of art there—characters based on superheroes and Kirby, a video game character. She sold two sizes of prints, plus buttons. Then a couple of months after that she set up at a Star Wars-themed convention held the weekend of May 4th ("may the forth be with you"). Again, she did well and most important, she was getting great support from the other vendors, who even gave her other ideas, like making holiday ornaments with her characters on them.

I belong to a cribbage group and we identify ourselves as "skunks"—as in "you've been skunked," which means you've been beaten by a lot of points. One day I was bragging about my daughter and her art, and another woman asked if she did custom work. I said sure, so the woman emailed Cosette and they took it from there. She came up with several designs for us, and we ended up not only with a logo, but also with personalized t-shirts!

Just the other day she got an email from a man in Los Angeles—somebody who heard about her from a friend who knows my brother. He has a software company and needs a logo. Cosette sent the man six quick sketches. He approved the first round and wants her to fill them in and they'll go from there.

One other place she's displaying and selling her work is at our small local used bookstore. The owner offered to let her have some space to put out "art cards"—they're drawings of cats and dinosaurs on greeting cards that are blank inside. She sells them for just $1.00 each or five for $4.00. It's not a lot, but it gets her face known and some sell every week.

She and I both keep our eyes open for opportunities. We're open to just about anything to get her exposure and experience. In the meantime, she's busy studying design at our community college. By the time she graduates she'll have a portfolio and a history of sales.

Cosette now produces many different types of art. This gargoyle was drawn when she was 17.

Social and Community Connection

By definition, autism is marked by impaired social communication, yet it by no means precludes meaningful interpersonal attachments. In order for kids with autism to grow into adults who are able to create and maintain some sort of social and community connection, however, parents and other adults once again usually need to provide the initial pushes.

While many factors contribute to a young adult's social participation, at least one study found that having parents who advocated for it was one of the primary determinants. Many teens on the spectrum do not reach out to others, and thus limit their opportunities for social success. Others, left to their own devices, actively avoid or pull back when others make advances. Therefore, parents are wise to create and push their teens into more active roles in social settings.

Marina, now 33, says one of her biggest mistakes was isolating herself throughout childhood.

> Throughout my childhood, I rarely enjoyed playing with other children. I preferred to be alone, and even when I was physically in the presence of others, my mind was far off. This behavior continued well into adulthood and I missed out on a lot of experiences and emotional growth. Although I feel most comfortable when alone, I have come to realize that extended periods of isolation breed depression, and heighten anxiety. If I had made more of an effort to socialize or leave the house when I was younger, perhaps I would not have been so depressed and anxious.
>
> I have learned that even though isolating myself can be rewarding, it is not necessarily the best move to make on a consistent basis. Sometimes we have to move out of our comfort zones and do what is healthy for ourselves and not just what feels good. I have learned since then that when one faces one's fears it only makes one stronger.

There are many factors that can make it difficult for a child to independently create successful social connections. From their earliest playground days, they are often more interested in noticing and managing their sensory worlds than their social ones. Young NT children tend to have loud, high-pitched voices that can actually be painful to kids with autism. They may also intrude in personal space in a way that is frightening or frustrating. If an autistic child doesn't understand how to communicate their distress, they're likely to hit, bite, or run away. The other kids notice and avoid them in the future.

Once enrolled in a classroom setting, sensory overload usually increases, especially at recess and lunch, the very time periods that NT children are forging and practicing friendships. If they do approach their peers, they often do it awkwardly, and focus on their special interests. Left on their own to figure it out, most children with autism are unable to salvage these already damaged interactions.

Step In Early and Be "Hands On"

Sensitive teachers and parents who step in at this early age can help. Finding a particularly nurturing child to serve as "helpmate" may work. These are often girls in the classroom who enjoying "mothering" a vulnerable child. Outside the classroom, parents can invite just one other preselected child to their home and provide a structure that offers more comfort than free play.

Cossette mentioned two experiences that helped her connect with peers. They highlight the importance of using a child's special interests as a social bridge whenever possible, and the role a teacher can play in a child's acceptance.

> While my elementary school years were the most difficult, due to lack of understanding from most of my teachers, there were some bright spots. In third grade all the kids wanted me to draw for them. That felt good and gave me a way to fit in more. Then in sixth grade, my teacher, Mrs. Warner, was the one who understood autism the most. She educated the other kids about what I had. Then the kids didn't try to bully me or mock me for my erratic behavior like I had experienced in earlier years. Now they were on my side and supported me throughout that year.

Sometimes changing schools, generally to one with smaller classes, helps not only academically but also socially. Scott was bored reading the "Goosebumps" series, and he refused to do the worksheets about the chapters. He liked to read, but he needed more hands-on work. His mother found another school that was project-oriented.

If they were learning about Russia, they'd have the kids cook Russian food and sing Russian songs. It was a smaller school and the kids got to know him better. They did more projects together. The kids accepted him more. It was the perfect place for him. That's where he found his two best friends.

Children on the spectrum need to be taught the social graces that other children pick up by observation and intuition. All children need reminders of basics, such as saying "please" and "thank you" and not chewing with your mouth open. But most NT kids figure out by themselves that these behaviors are unacceptable. They actively look to the faces of others for feedback and they adjust their behavior to elicit approval and praise. Autistic children often miss this or simply don't care enough to change unless there are concrete negative consequences beyond nonverbal disapproval.

A child with autism needs clear, concise rules for social engagement. Breaking the rule must result in a negative consequence 100% of the time so that good habits are established.

Create Games That Teach—Examples from Scott's Mom

Parents or other adults can create games that teach social skills such as turn taking. Scott's mother, who taught after-dinner clean-up skills on Saturday nights, also used that evening for practicing both conversational and behavioral turn taking.

We practiced conversational turn taking during dinner. We each took a turn talking about any challenges that were coming up for each person the following week. Everyone had to listen quietly and carefully so that they could then create a prayer for that person.

After dinner was finished and the kids completed clean-up chores, we often played games. When Scott was younger he didn't handle losing well. We started with simple games like 'go fish' and later moved to more complex ones like Scrabble and Clue and so on. I knew he had to learn to lose gracefully.

Scott's story also highlights how important, in multiple realms, siblings can be in helping a child on the spectrum.

> Scott was born three months premature and we didn't know if he would live, much less go to college. He was on a ventilator and in neo-natal intensive care for two months. He almost didn't make it several times. Scott has a brother just 18 months older, and he pulled Scott along through preschool and elementary school. Scott was motivated to keep up with him, so he was always reaching. They both loved to read and play Legos.

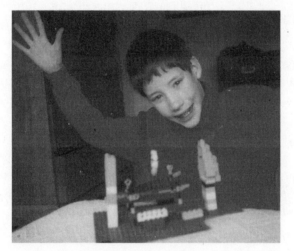

Scott, age 10, being creative with Legos.

Scott also had a younger sister, Katie. His mother believes that by being five years younger, she provided a different perspective, and was also helpful by anticipating and helping prevent social mishaps.

> Katie helped Scott realize he was better at things than she was, and that made him feel secure. I think other children in a family can sometimes be just as effective as a therapist, because they speak up, give feedback, motivate, and have their sibling's back.

How to Find Activities Outside School

Structured social activities outside the home are usually more rewarding than unstructured play or classroom social life. These activities might involve the child's special interests or expose them to new interests they would otherwise never have developed. Examples are extracurricular classes, boys or girls clubs, church youth groups, camps, or professionally facilitated social skills groups.

One well-known organization that has been intensely scrutinized is 4-H, America's largest youth development and youth mentoring organization. While some people still associate this program with rural communities and activities, it is actually found in every county in the United States, and has programs in science and technology, health, citizenship, and mentoring.

Researchers began following 4-H participants in a longitudinal study that began in 2002 and was repeated annually for eight years, surveying over 7,000 teens from diverse background. Compared to their peers, these youth were four times more likely to later make contributions to their community, twice as likely to make healthier life choices, and twice as likely to participate in extracurricular science, engineering, and computer technology programs. Girls in their last year of high school who were in 4-H were three times as likely to participate in extracurricular science programs. It is clear that this program's structured learning and adult mentoring helps participants create successful lives. It may be a great fit for some children on the spectrum, since their special interest may fall within one of the organization's specific tracks. For example, their science track includes choices from robotics to filmmaking to engineering and small engine projects.

Non-Competitive Group Activities Strengthen Confidence

Other programs that focus on non-competitive recreational activities can sometimes be a great fit for teens on the spectrum. Ballroom dancing is one example. It is ritualized, and there are rules to follow both for dance movements and social interaction. Another option that is readily available is karate classes.

Daniel enjoyed karate and also participated in several social groups. Even though he had four siblings, his parents thought he needed to be exposed to peers outside the family. He and his mother both think the activities helped.

I think having Dan active in church activities and Boy Scouts did the most to prepare him for adulthood. The adults knew about his needs and were very supportive. He also went to a therapy center that ran social-relational support groups. His therapist and some of her employees provided excellent groups where Dan was able to have friends and progress socially.

Daniel, practicing karate at age eight, and in his high school graduation portrait.

As children enter their teens, if they have not had success in earlier years, they may have by now decided to remain loners. High school can be a social nightmare for many teens with autism. They are typically not interested in the usual dramas that continually play out at this age. They may or may not want to date, but usually lack awareness of the nuances of "playing the dating game." They miss indirect communication and innuendo, which for NT teens comprises the bulk of flirting behavior.

This is a prime time for parents to step in and provide alternative, positive experiences for their teen. Again, this takes a loving push and may meet with resistance. It can also be scary for the parent. Scott's mom said she knew she had to transition her son into a more independent role before he left for college.

I knew it was going to be hard for him to live away from home. I knew I had to transition out of the role of the person he always went to with problems. So we sent him to church camps in the summer and had him spend weekends away with other kids. And then we had him go to England for a summer program. I was terrified! But I knew it was a well-structured program and he'd get to study things he liked, like medieval history and architecture. It turned out successful but it wasn't easy on any of us at first.

College can be a new social beginning for some. Scott's roommate, who was aware of Scott's diagnosis, was a key to his successful entry into adulthood. Both Scott and his dad are appreciative and grateful for the relationship that developed. The two participated in numerous activities together and joined a prayer group every Saturday night.

Romantic Relationships and Marriage

Some individuals on the spectrum are not interested in romantic relationships. They may, like Temple, have never had the urge to date, or even experienced a crush on anyone. They find life fulfilling without marriage, children, or a committed partner.

Others on the spectrum, much as some NT youth, are ambivalent about a serious relationship or marriage. They may find that social anxiety makes introductions and interactions frightening. If they are not in college or the workplace, they may not have many opportunities to meet others. If their special interests are solitary, this further increases their odds of being alone.

Individuals on the spectrum often find it easier to relate either to others on or at the edge of the spectrum, or from another culture. This makes sense, because social missteps may go unnoticed and routine NT romantic interactions such as flirting may not be expected. Partnerships of those on the spectrum may also involve a greater age difference than typical. This too makes sense, as many on the spectrum relate better to others either younger or older than themselves versus same-age peers.

For those on the spectrum who do want to marry, live with someone, or otherwise be in a serious committed relationship, a common route to finding a partner is through academic or workplace proximity, shared interests, or shared activities.

Marina and Sarah both fit this pattern. Marina met her husband at college, while Sarah met her future husband at work. Both men were initially in positions of relative authority to the women, and Sarah's husband is 16 years her senior. Each couple shared common special interests, which were the centerpiece of many of their conversations. Neither woman was intent on "dating" in the traditional sense of trying out multiple partners; they met and liked their future husbands and bonded as they realized they had similar values, and could be themselves in the relationship.

Marina met her husband at Bible college, where he was an instructor. He had given her his business card because he was also selling life insurance and financial products. What began as a rather unorthodox initiation by Marina quickly developed into a friendship and later a romantic relationship that led to marriage and parenthood.

> One night I was having trouble sleeping, there was nothing useful on TV, and I was really bored. I noticed his business card on the table so I called the number. He asked me why I was calling him so late and I told him that I was bored, and we started conversing from there.
>
> The next day we spent some time together and a friendship developed rather quickly. It was not something I thought about or even wanted to happen; it just did. We spent a lot of time together going to the park and for walks.
>
> Both of us were interested in the Bible and I had studied it extensively, so many of our conversations were more like me giving him theology lectures.

Sarah met her husband through her special interest and vocation in wildlife biology. He was a speaker at meetings and workshops she attended, and they got to know each other further while working on a project together.

> We talked on radios to each other all day while we were monitoring two pairs of nesting Swanson's Hawks. His humor, kindness, and unselfishness, not to mention his good looks, attracted me. He gave me his email address and I later told my boss how much I liked him. I believe she told him to ask me out. After a month of periodic emails,

we began talking on the phone. After we again worked together, I suggested we do something socially. We met for an opera concert performance and began dating exclusively in the fall of 2007.

We knew after two months that we had the same values, like kindness, honesty, and loyalty, and the same interests, like wildlife, animals, and traveling. In 2009 I moved in with him, we got engaged the next year, and were married in 2012. We are doing well.

When Sarah and Marina were asked what advice they would have for others on the spectrum who are interested in building relationships, their statements were similar. They stressed the need for both self-awareness and self-acceptance. They also highlighted the vital role of shared interests and activities. Sarah advised parents to be supportive and encourage their kids to be patient and to do social activities. She also had some suggestions about how to navigate the social interactions.

Don't call or contact someone you like too much just after meeting them, and instead email or text them patiently. Remember to share in conversations. A good guide is to offer two or three sentences, and then wait and allow the other person to enter into the conversation. Remember to ask questions about the other person and to not overwhelm them with too much detail. Getting to know someone requires patience in discussions.

Enjoy and be comfortable being alone with yourself, and know which qualities you don't want, and those you do want and like in a person. Try to express those qualities yourself and find peace with those qualities. Let go of the immediate and urgent need to have a significant other. Find interests and hobbies that include interacting with people and are social, and be receptive to meeting people and developing relationships like friendships. They may later possibly become romantic.

Marina echoed similar wisdom:

As for advice, the first step to developing a relationship with someone is to be present. Involving yourself in activities will allow you to meet more people. The more people you meet, the more likely you are to find someone you like and who likes you.

Also, it is imperative to just be yourself because ultimately it is you who the other person will end up with, and you want someone to like and appreciate you for who you really are. It is also important to like yourself. If you do not like yourself, you will make it difficult for others to like you. If you love and appreciate yourself, others will be able to witness the best of you and are more likely to mirror your feelings.

Lastly, do not be afraid to take chances such as giving someone a call, attending that party or event, or enrolling into that class. You have to give people opportunities to get to know you. Make yourself known by being present.

Volunteering Is Good for Your Kid: Some Examples

Many of the people profiled for this book were exposed to volunteer work or community participation as children or teens. They, as well as their parents, all reported benefits.

One mother, whose 26-year-old daughter didn't opt to provide a profile but gave permission for her mom to contribute, related this valuable learning experience she created for her child.

> I took her from a young age to volunteer at homeless shelters. She would never have done this on her own, but I wanted her to get used to it. So when she was around 11 she would go with me and we would take food and clothes out to the river, where the homeless often stayed. It was her job to gather all the clothes and sort them by size and color. She was very serious about helping people find "nice" outfits that looked good on them. She also worked from a young age in the church.

Research on the effects of volunteering tell us that there are individual benefits to be derived from doing volunteer work that reach far beyond the volunteer act itself. These effects may linger long after the volunteer role is finished. A number of studies show that there are physical health benefits to volunteering. It's possible that volunteering may be particularly empowering for those on the autism spectrum who are isolated, as one study found that volunteering had its strongest positive impact on people who otherwise reported the least number of social activities.

Another study found that the teens who volunteered reported increased awareness of themselves and others, in addition to the new skills they learned. Their parents reported that their children were more willing to make decisions after being volunteers.

Several of the people profiled here in fact volunteered past adolescence into adulthood. Examples include Patrick doing recordings for the blind, Martha having worked with the state fair and ushering at her church, and Marina feeding the homeless and working with the SPCA. Being a positive force in someone's life, according to Marina, simply makes her "feel really good."

Feeling good and doing well—what more could we want for our children? By providing ongoing loving pushes, and teaching vital life skills, our ASD kids will be well positioned to become successful adults.

FINAL THOUGHTS

Youth on the autism spectrum are in great need of our guidance as they transition into adulthood. Worldwide, increasing numbers of families and professionals are discovering that these kids are not well prepared or ready for this next stage of life. This is alarming not only for our children, but also for parents, and for society.

There are several reasons this is happening, and we can change most of them. Two classic aspects of autism are social impairment and a tendency to restrict interests and behaviors. These traits combine to create tremendous obstacles for many ASD teens on the brink of independence. They are compounded by historical changes in culture, parenting, and technology. We now have a perfect storm for high functioning ASD youth to falter, perform well below their capabilities, and remain dependent on their parents well past the age that they're capable of being independent.

It's up to parents, teachers, professionals, and "the village" to help this struggling group. We must provide, as early as possible, frequent and consistent "loving pushes" to help our kids keep moving forward. We can't expect them to do it alone. Children on the spectrum rely on what others in their environment expose them to. We can't wait for them to ask, or to express interest. It may never happen.

We must advocate for educational systems to return to valuing hands-on vocational classes, because some individuals on the spectrum, as well as some NT kids, could excel and enjoy them. Many children who in years past would have found work in the trades come out of high school with no exposure at all to these options. If they are not introduced to these options, either by a parent, teacher, or mentor, they are highly unlikely to discover them on their own.

Our children need step-by-step practical help more than they need sheltering. They, like all children, need to be held accountable at their level of capability. Holding them back because of a label hurts them in the end. We can support and accommodate their needs without depriving them of life struggles that everyone necessarily goes through to grow.

Technology has penetrated our lives, and we're beginning to realize how this affects those on the autism spectrum. With brains already wired for relentless and exacting logic, plus vulnerability to social and sensory overload, it makes sense that children on the spectrum are more susceptible to technology's negative aspects. The Internet and video games, especially role-playing ones, can become rapidly compelling to the point of addiction for many of our youth, especially males.

Parents and educators need to wake up to this danger. Technology use must be strictly monitored and only used to strengthen our children by exposing them to a wider, not a more narrow, world. The Internet is like a vast, lush garden. It contains healthy, beautiful flowers, and you'll sometimes find extraordinary and rare butterflies in it. But it also contains weeds and lots of dirt and nasty stuff. Kids play in dirt. ASD kids too often play in the dirt on the Internet, and then they stay there so long it becomes their world.

We realize it's difficult for some parents to "push" their children, especially when the kids resist (as they usually do), everyone is tired, and the outcome is not guaranteed. But it's one of the greatest gifts anyone can give a child. Without it, for far too many ASD youth, the outcome *is* predictable: continued dependency, vulnerability to internet/gaming addiction, loneliness, and insecurity, and a vocational wasteland.

We hope the individuals who generously shared their real stories in this book provided insight into how important loving pushes can be. We hope they gave you the courage to step up and lovingly push the ASD youth in your life, whether you're a parent, teacher, neighbor, friend, minister, or counselor. They deserve it and we owe it to them.

ACKNOWLEDGEMENTS

First, I owe tremendous thanks and gratitude to Temple Grandin. Her laser-sharp insight and intelligence, her passion for helping others on the spectrum, her amazing stamina, and her wicked sense of humor made it a joy to collaborate on this project. Thanks also to her assistant, Cheryl Miller.

Second, major thanks to Scott, Marina, Jaime, Martha, Cosette, Daniel, Sarah, and Patrick, the eight individuals profiled in this book. Sharing their personal journeys was a generous gift. Their desire to unselfishly help others was inspiring.

Special thanks to Lynne Weissman, parent pioneer and cofounder of the Sacramento AS Information & Support Group in 1995. Many of those profiled shared their stories after reading about this project in the group's newsletter.

Thanks to Katie & Doug, Loretta, Maria, Stephanie, Nancy & John, Armida, Mrs. Letsos, Mr. Shanks, Gin & Ray, Mary, Cammie, Barbara, Cara, Dawn, Dan, Michelle, and Duane, who added to the stories or contributed anecdotes from their own lives.

Sincere thanks also to Drs. Kimberly Young, Mark Klinger, Hilarie Cash, Andrew Doan, Jennifer Neitzel, and Theodore Henderson, as well as to Paul Johnson, M.A., Jason Rohrer, Regine Pfeiffer, and Christopher Mulligan, LCSW.

Liz Woolley is owed particular gratitude for allowing us to tell her son Shawn's story, and for continuing to help others find support and help.

Dr. James Cooper, psychologist, poet, and friend, came up with *The Loving Push*, a title that all immediately agreed was perfect. He also reviewed sections of the manuscript, adding clarity and precision.

I thank my former students and interns, who remarked "you need to write a book" so often that apparently it was destined to manifest. Thank you for your trust in my ability to have something worth saying. Additionally, patients and their families have been among my finest teachers. I am grateful to each of them.

Finally, thank you to Future Horizons and their great team, including Robert Morrow, who brilliantly captured the essence of *The Loving Push* in his cover design, and John Yacio, for graphic design. Finally, I'd like to thank Wayne Gilpin, head honcho, who embraced this project with enthusiasm from day one. His publishing smarts are equaled only by his dedication to the autism community and his personal strength, humor, and tenacity.

—*Debra Moore, Ph.D.*

I want to thank my coauthor Debra Moore for all her hard work on this book and for finding all the people who told their stories. Without Debra's assistance this book would not have been possible.

—*Temple Grandin, Ph.D.*

REFERENCES

Introduction

Roux, Anne M., Shattuck, Paul T., Rast, Jessica E., Rava, Julianna A., and Anderson, Kristy, A. National Autism Indicators Report: Transition into Young Adulthood. Philadelphia, PA: Life Course Outcomes Research Program, A.J. Drexel Autism Institute, Drexel University, 2015. Accessed 08-14-15 http://drexel.edu/autisminstitute/research-projects/research/ResearchProgramin-LifeCourseOutcomes/IndicatorsReport/#sthash.b8EVdh9b.dpuf.

Silberman, Steve. (2015). *NeuroTribes: The Legacy of Autism and the Future of Neurodiversity.* New York, NY: Avery (Penguin/Random House).

Chapter 1

The profiles in this chapter were obtained in one of two ways. A few of the individuals were already known to Debra as previous clients who had seen her or someone at her clinic for counseling or diagnostic evaluation or participated in group meetings. Others were solicited via a group email graciously sent by Lynne Weisman, parent of a child on the spectrum and Autism Spectrum Consultant & Co-Founder of Sacramento Asperger Syndrome Information & Support Groups.

Chapter 2

Seligman, Martin (1998). *Learned Optimism*. New York, NY: Pocket Books.

Seligman, M.E.P, and Maier, S.F. (1967) Failure to escape traumatic shock. *Journal of Experimental Psychology 74*, 1-9.

Hagner, D., Kurtz, A., Cloutier, H., Arakelian, C., Brucker, D.L., & May, J. (2012). Outcomes of a family-centered transition process for students with autism spectrum disorders. *Focus on Autism and Other Developmental Disabilities, 27*(1), 42-50. doi: 10/1177/1088357611430841

Chapter 3

Brown, Brené (2102). *Daring Greatly: How the Courage to be Vulnerable Transforms the Way We Live, Love, Parent, and Lead.* New York, NY: Gotham Books.

Snyder, C.R., Ilardi, Stephen S., Cheavens, Jen, Michael, Scott T., Yamhure, Laura, & Sympson, Susie. (2000) The Role of Hope in Cognitive-Behavior Therapies. *Cognitive Therapy and Research, 270 (6)*, 747–762.

Chapter 5

Strang, J. F., Kenworthy, L., Daniolos, P., Case, L., Wills, M. C., Martin, A., & Wallace, G. L. (2012). Depression and Anxiety Symptoms in Children and Adolescents with Autism Spectrum Disorders without Intellectual Disability. *Research in Autism Spectrum Disorders, 6*(1), 406–412. Retrieved from doi:10.1016/j.rasd.2011.06.015

Sterzing, Paul R, Shattack, Paul T., Narendorf, Sarah C., Wagner, Mary, & Cooper, Benjamin P. (2012) Bullying Involvement and Autism Spectrum Disorders: Prevalence and Correlates of Bullying Involvement Among Adolescents With an Autism Spectrum Disorder. *Archives of Pediatric Adolescent Medicine, 166* (11), 1058-1064. Retrieved 08/14/2015 from: http://archpedi.jamanetwork.com/article.aspx?articleid=1355390

References

Little, Liza. (2001) Peer victimization of children with Asperger spectrum disorders. *Journal of the American Academy of Child Adolescent Psychiatry. 40*(9), 995-996.

Cappadocia, M. C., Weiss, J. A., & Pepler, D. (2012). Bullying Experiences among Children and Youth with Autism Spectrum Disorders. *Journal of Autism and Developmental Disorders, 42*(2), 266-277.

Wood B., Rea M.S., Plitnick B, & Figueiro M.G. (2013) Light level and duration of exposure determine the impact of self-luminous tablets on melatonin suppression. *Applied Ergonomics, 44* (2), 237-240. Retrieved 7-2-2015 from http://www.ncbi.nlm.nih.gov/pubmed/22850476

Cohen, Simonne, Conduit, Russell, Lockley, Steven W., Rajaratnam, Shantha, & Cornish, Kim M. (2014) The relationship between sleep and behavior in autism spectrum disorder (ASD): A review. *Journal of Neurodevelopmental Disorders, 6* (44). Retrieved 7-2-2015 from: http://www.jneurodevdisorders.com/content/6/1/44

Ratey, John J. (2009) *Spark: The Revolutionary New Science of Exercise and the Brain.* New York: Little, Brown and Company.

Goines, P., and Van de Water, J. (2010) The Immune System's Role in the Biology of Autism. *Current Opinion in Neurology, 23*(2), 111-117.

Whipple, Jennifer. (2004) Music in Intervention for Children and Adolescents with Autism: A Meta-Analysis. *Journal of Music Therapy, 41*(2), 90-106.

De Hert, M, et al. (2011) Metabolic and endocrine adverse effects of second-generation antipsychotics in children and adolescents: A systematic review of randomized, placebo controlled trials and guidelines for clinical practice. *European Psychiatry 26*(3), 144-158.

Vitiello, B., et al. (2009) Antipsychotics in children and adolescents: Increasing use, evidence for efficacy and safety concerns, *European Neuropsychopharmacology, 19* (9), 1-7. Retrieved 8-14-2015 from https://www.ecnp.eu/~/media/Files/ecnp/communication/talk-of-the-month/Celso%20Arango/110303%20 paper%20Arango%20Antipsychotics%20in%20children%20and%20adolescents%20increasing%20use%20evidence.pdf

Anderson, Goerge M et ct. (2007) Effects of Short- and Long-Term Risperidone Treatment on Prolactin Levels in Children with Autism. *Biological Psychiatry. 61,* 545-550.

Jane A. Foster and Karen-Anne McVey Neufeld (2013) Gut–brain axis: how the microbiome influences anxiety and depression. *Trends in Neurosciences 36*, 305-312.

Gilbert, Jack A., Krajmalnik-Brown, Rosa, Porazinska, Dorota L, Weiss, Sophie J., and Knight, Rob. (2013). Toward Effective Probiotics for Autism and Other Neurodevelopmental Disorders. *Cell 155* (7): 1446-1448.

Messaoudi, Michael, Lalonde, Robert, Violle, Nicolas, Javelot, Hervé, Desor, Didier, Nejdi, Amine, Bisson, Jean-Françoisn, Rougeot, Catherine, Pichelin, Matthieu, Cazaubiel, Murielle & Cazaubiel, Jean-Marc. (2011). Assessment of psychotropic-like properties of a probiotic formulation (Lactobacillus helveticus R0052 and Bifidobacterium longum R0175) in rats and human subjects. *British Journal of Nutrition 105*, 755–764.

Chapter 6

American Academy of Pediatrics (2013). *Children, Adolescents, and the Media* (Policy Statement) Downloaded 08/14/2015 from http://pediatrics.aappublications.org/content/early/2013/10/24/peds.2013-2656

ZERO TO THREE (2014) *Screen Sense: Setting the Record Straight: Research-Based Guidelines for Screen Use for Children Under 3 Years Old.* Georgetown Early Learning Project at Georgetown University. Lerner, Claire Lerner, and Barr, Rachel. Downloaded 08/11/2015 from http://www.zerotothree.org/parenting-resources/screen-sense/screen-sense_wp_final3.pdf

Gentile, D.A., Oberg, C., & Sherwood, N.E. (2004)Well-child visits in the video age: pediatricians and the American Academy of Pediatrics' guidelines for children's media use. *Pediatrics, 114* (5), 1235 -1241.

References

Shane, H. & Albert, P.D. (2008). Electronic Screen Media For Persons with Autism Spectrum Disorders: Results of a Survey. *Journal of Autism and Developmental Disorders 38*, 1495-1508. Accessed 07/01/2016 at http://link.springer.com/article/10.1007/s10803-007-0527-5#page-2

Finkenauer, Catrin et al. (2012) Brief Report: Examining the Link between Autistic Tratins and Compulsive Internet Use in a Non-Clinical Sample. *Journal of Autism and Developmental Disorders 42*,1465. Accessed 07-01-2015 at http://link.springer.com/article/10.1007/s10803-012-1465-4/fulltext.html

Mazurek, Micah O., Engelhardt, Christopher R. (2013) Video game use and problem behaviors in boys with autism spectrum disorders. *Research in Autism Spectrum Disorders 7* (2), 316-324. Accessed online 07-01-2015 at http://pediatrics.aappublications.org/content/132/2/260.full

MacMullin J.A., Lanky, Y., Weiss J.A. (2015) Plugged in: Electronics use in youth and young adults with autism spectrum disorder. *Autism, 18*, 1-10. Downloaded 06-28-2015 from aut.sagepub.com DOI:10.1177/1362361314566047

Brand, Matthias, Young, Kimberly S, & Laier, Christian. (2014) Prefrontal control and Internet addiction: a theoretical model and review of neuropsychological and neuroimaging findings. *Frontiers in Human Neuroscience. 8*, 1-12. Downloaded 06-28-2015 from www.frontiersin.org/article/10.3389/fnhum.2014.00375/full

Maguire E.A., Woollett, K., Spiers, H.J. (2006) London taxi drivers and bus drivers: a structural MRI and neuropsychological analysis. *Hippocampus, 16*, (12), 1091-1101.

Elbert,T., Pantev, C., Wienbruch, C., Rockstroh, B., & Taub, E. (1995). Increased cortical representation of the fingers of the left hand in string players. *Science, 270*, 305–307. Accessed 06-29-2015 from http://kops.uni-konstanz.de/bitstream/handle/123456789/10711/Elbert_1995_Increased_Cortical_Representation.pdf?sequence=1

Wang H., Jin C., Yuan K., Shakir T.M., Mao C., Niu X., Niu C., Guo L, & Zhang, M. (2015) The alteration of gray matter volume and cognitive control in adolescents with internet gaming disorder. *Frontiers in Behavioral Neuroscience, 20*, (9), 1-7.

Mulligan, Christopher. (2013) The toxic relationship: Autism and technology. Accessed 07-03-2015 from http://www.groupworkswest.com/the-toxic-connection-autism-and-technology/ and via phone call with author.

http://www.cdc.gov/ncbddd/autism/data.html

http://www.digitaltrends.com/gaming/the-history-of-the-xbox/

http://www.geek.com/games/playstation-2-hits-us-today-564850/

Doan, Andrew, and Strickland, Brooke. (2012). *Hooked on Games: The Lure and Cost of Video Game and Internet Addiction*. [Kindle].

Voss, A., Cash, H., Hurdiss, S., Bishop, F., Clam, W., & Doan, A. (2105) Case Report: Internet Gaming Disorder Associated With Pornography Use. *Yale Journal of Biology and Medicine, 88*, 1-6.

Kim, Junghyun, & Haridakis, Paul M. (2009) The role of internet user characteristics and motives in explaining three dimensions of Internet addiction. *Journal of Computer-Mediated Communication, 14*, 988–1015. Downloaded 07/01/2015 from http://onlinelibrary.wiley.com/doi/10.1111/j.1083-6101.2009.01478.x/full

Young KISS., Rodgers R.C. (1998) The relationship between depression and Internet addiction. *Cyber Psychology and Behavior 1*: 25–28.

Lemans, J.S., Valkenbur, P.M., & Peter, J. (2011) Psychosocial causes and consequences of pathological. *Computers in Human Behavior*. 27, 144-152.

Wei, H.T., Chen, M.H., Huang, P.C., & Bai, Y.M. (2012) The association between online gaming, social phobia, and depression: an Internet survey. *BMC Psychiatry 28*, Accessed 06-28-2015 http://www.biomedcentral.com/1471-244X/12/92

Gnash, S.,van Schie H.T., de Lange F.P., Thompson E., & Wigboldus, D.H. (2012) How the human brain goes virtual: distinct cortical regions of the person-processing network are involved in self-identification with virtual agents. *Cerebral Cortex 22* (7) 1577-1585. Downloaded 07/01/2015 from http://cercor.oxfordjournals.org/content/22/7/1577.long

References

Volkmar, F. R, & Cohen, D. J. (1991) Comorbid association of autism and schizophrenia. *American Journal of Psychiatry*. 148,1705–1707.

Personal phone call with Liz Woolley July 27, 2015

(2014, May 7) The Beginning: Interview with Liz Woolley about video game addiction, her son Shawn Woolley, and why she founded On-Line Gamers Anonymous Retrieved from www.youtube.com/watch?v=QJKSYxt_pVg

Gartner, Inc. (2011). Gartner Spending on Gaming to Exceed $74 Billion in 2011 (Press Release) Retrieved from www.gartner.com/newsroom/id/1737414

http://www.turtle-entertainment.com/news/esl-to-create-anti-ped-esports-policy-with-support-of-nada/ Accessed 8-17-2015

Rose, Mike. (2013) Understanding the realities of video game monetization. http://www.gamasutra.com/view/news/205412/Understanding_the_realities_of_video_game_monetization.php. Accessed 8-10-2015

Ambinder, Mike. (undated PowerPoint slides) Valve's Approach to Playtesting: The Application of Empiricism. Accessed 08/11/2015 from http://www.valvesoftware.com/publications/2009/GDC2009ValvesApprochToPlaytesting.pdf

Ferrara, John (Interviewer) & Ambinder, Mike (Interviewee). (2012) *Interview with Mike Ambinder of Valve Software*. http://rosenfeldmedia.com/playful-design/interview-with-mike-ambinder-0/ Accessed 8-11-2015

Game balancing and monetization (Julian Hühnermann, Head of Publisher Relations, Gratispay / Balao GmbH) Conference schedule downloaded 08-01-2015 from http://www.mmofacts.com/blog/browsergames-forum-2009-program-revealed-6739

http://www.regine-pfeiffer.de, translated by Manfred Schropp. Accessed 07-28-2015

http://amraverlag.e-bookshelf.de/products/reading-epub/product-id/3632845/title/Internet-%2Bund%2BComputersucht.html. Accessed 07-29-2015

http://www.independent.co.uk/life-style/gadgets-and-tech/news/video-gamers-to-be-tested-for-doping-after-player-admits-we-were-all-on-adderall-10415509.html

Zhan Ye, http://www.slideshare.net/vgsummit/zhan-ye-what-us-game-developers-need-to-know-about-freetoplay-in-china-2408412. Accessed 08-16-2015

Personal email sent 08-03-2015 to Debra Moore

Personal communication (phone call) 08-22-2015 with Debra Moore

Mazurek, Micah O, Christopher R. Engelhardt, Kelsey E. Clark. (2015). Video games from the perspective of adults with autism spectrum. *Computers in Human Behavior, 51*,122-130.

Engelhardt CR, Mazurek MO.(2014) *Autism, 18* (5):529-37. Video game access, parental rules, and problem behavior: a study of boys with autism spectrum disorder.

Kimberly S. Young, PhD CBT-IA: The First Treatment Model for Internet Addiction. *Journal of Cognitive Psychotherapy: An International Quarterly* V25, #4, 2011

Brand, Matthias, Young, Kimberly S, & Laier, Christian. (2014) Prefrontal control and Internet addiction: a theoretical model and review of neuropsychological and neuroimaging findings. *Frontiers in Human Neuroscience. 8*, 1-12.

Han, D.H., Hwang, J.W., & Renshaw, P.F. (2010) Bupropion Sustained Release Treatment Decreases Craving for Video Games and Cue-Induced Brain Activity in Patients with Internet Video Game Addiction. *Experimental and Clinical Psychopharmacology, 18* (4) 297-304.

https://www.aspiescentral.com/threads/i-can-help-some-of-you.12775/#post-239746. Accessed 8-10-15 and via personal email

Personal phone call with Dr. H. Cash 08-18-2015

The website for the ReStart Program is: http://www.netaddictionrecovery.com

Cash, Hilarie and McDaneil, Kim (2008) *Video Games & Your Kids: How Parents Stay in Control.* Enumclaw WA: Issues Press.

Phone call with Paul MA, LMHCA Behavioral Specialist, Mindfulness Practitioner 08-20-2015

Chapter 7

Phone call with Dr. Mark Klinger 07-24-2015

Huang, Patty MD et al. (2012) Factors Associated with Driving in Teens with Autism Spectrum Disorders. *Journal of Developmental and Behavioral Pediatrics, 33* (1), 70-74.

(new format) Wehman, P., Schall, C., McDonough, J., Molinelli, A., Riehle, E., Ham, W., & Thiss, W. R. (2013). Project SEARCH for youth with autism spectrum disorders: Increasing competitive employment on transition from high school. *Journal of Positive Behavior Interventions, 15*(3), 144-155. doi: 10.1177/1098300712459760.

http://www.cdc.gov/motorvehiclesafety/teen_drivers/teendrivers_factsheet.html

Tyler, S. (2013) Asperger's Syndrome: The implications for driver training methods and road safety. Highlands Drive Safe, member of ADTA and ACRS. *Journal of the Australasian College of Road Safety, 24* (1) 55-62.

Shatyermman, O. (2007). Peer victimization in adolescents and young adults diagnosed with Asperger's syndrome: A link to depressive symptomatology, anxiety symptomatology and suicidal ideation. *Issues in Comprehensive Pediatric Nursing, 30*, (3), 87-107.

Howard, B., Cohn, E., & Orsmond, G. (2006). Understanding and negotiating friendships: Perspectives from an adolescent with Asperger syndrome. *Autism, 10* (6), 619-627.

Orsmond, G. L., Krauss, M. W., & Seltzer, M. M. (2004). Peer relationships and social and recreational activities among adolescents and adults with autism. *Journal of Autism and Developmental Disorders, 34* (3), 245–256.

Jeleicic, H., Bobek, D.L., Phelps, E., Lerner, R.M., & Lerner J.V. (2007) Using positive youth development to predict contribution and risk behaviors in early adolescence: Findings from the first two waves of the 4-H Study of Positive Youth Development. *International Journal of Behavioral Development, 31* (3),2623-273.

Liptak, Gregory S et al. (2011) Social Participation in a Nationally Representative Sample of Older Youth and Young Adults with Autism. *Journal of Developmental and Behavioral Pediatrics, 32* (4), 277-283.

Hamilton, Stephen, and Fenzel, L. Mickey. (1998) The Impact of Volunteer Experience on Adolescent Social Development: Evidence of Program Effects. *Journal of Adolescent Research, 3,* 65-80.

ADDITIONAL READING

Different...Not Less by Dr. Temple Grandin.

Fourteen fully verbal adults on the autism spectrum describe successful employment and how a diagnosis provided insight into social relationships.

The Way I See It by Dr. Temple Grandin

Great book for teachers and parents working with and/or parenting young children and includes updates on medications.

Thinking in Pictures by Dr. Temple Grandin

Explains visual thinking and she describe her experiences with the beneficial effects of anti-depressants for anxiety.

Unwritten Rules of Social Relationships: Decoding Social Mysteries through the Unique Perspectives of Autism by Dr. Temple Grandin and Sean Barron

Provides insight for teenagers and adults on understanding social relationship.

The Autistic Brain by Dr. Temple Grandin and Richard Panek

Matching the right jobs with people on the autism spectrum. Explains different types of specialized thinking such as photorealistic visual thinking, pattern/match thinking and word thinking.

Hope for the Violently Aggressive Child by Dr. Ralph Ankenman

Presents new diagnoses and treatment options for children who have severe disruptive meltdowns at home or school. Referred to as Immature Adrenaline Systems Overreactivity (IASO), this approach is based on the relationship between aggression and the body's adrenaline systems.

The Parents Guide to the Medical World of Autism by Edward, Aull, M.D.

When families are faced with a diagnosis of autism, they find themselves swimming in a vast sea of new terms and treatment options. Dr. Aull identifies the best and safest treatment strategies for your child's particular diagnosis.